# The Jason Porter Case

### *Love, Lies, and Heather Rovet's Fight for Justice*

Jimmie B. Wald

# Copyright page

All rights reserved. No part of this publication may be reproduced, distributed, or transmitted in any form or by any means, including photocopying, recording, or other electronic or mechanical methods, without the prior written permission of the publisher, except in the case of brief quotations embodied in critical reviews and certain other noncommercial uses permitted by copyright law.

Copyright © 2025, Jimmie B. Wald

# Disclaimer Page

This book is a work of nonfiction based on extensive research, interviews, and publicly available information. Every effort has been made to ensure the accuracy and reliability of the content. However, the author and publisher do not guarantee the completeness or correctness of all information presented.

Some events, conversations, and perspectives have been reconstructed or summarized for clarity and narrative flow. Names, dates, and details have been verified to the best of the author's ability but may be subject to differing accounts.

The author and publisher disclaim any liability for any errors, omissions, or outcomes resulting from the use of this material.

# Table of content

**Copyright page**..................................................................... 2

**Disclaimer Page**.................................................................. 3

**Introduction**........................................................................ 6

**Chapter One**...................................................................... 14
    The Making Of A Monster......................................... 14

**Chapter Two**...................................................................... 29
    Apprentice years......................................................... 29

**Chapter Three**................................................................... 44
    Digital Romeo............................................................. 44

**Chapter Four**..................................................................... 58
    Heather Rovet Story.................................................. 58

**Chapter Five**...................................................................... 71
    Three Years Of Lies.................................................... 71

**Chapter six**........................................................................ 84
    Unraveling................................................................... 84

**Chapter seven**.................................................................. 96

The Victim Network..................................................96

**Chapter Eight**............................................................... 108
   From Victim To Vigilante....................... 108

**Chapter Nine**.................................................................119
   Legal Labyrinth...................................... 119

**Chapter Ten**.................................................................. 130
   Psychology Of Predation...................... 130

**Chapter Eleven**.............................................................141
   Documentary Genesis........................... 141

**Chapter Twelve**........................................................... 152
   Dissecting The Documentary................152

**Chapter Thirteen**........................................................ 162
   Aftermath And Legacy.......................... 162

# Introduction

On a sunny morning in July 2018, Heather Rovet opened her front door expecting to see the same elderly handyman who had previously worked on her midtown Toronto condominium. Instead, she found herself face-to-face with a charismatic stranger whose salt-and-pepper hair and gap-toothed smile would soon become the centerpiece of one of Canada's most compelling true crime stories. The man introduced himself as Jace Peretti, and in that moment, neither Heather nor the broader Toronto community could have imagined that this seemingly innocent encounter would eventually expose a web of deception spanning over a decade.

What followed was a three-year relationship that Heather believed represented everything she had been searching for: genuine connection, emotional intimacy, and a partnership built on trust and shared dreams. Jace appeared to be the perfect companion—attentive without being overwhelming, successful without being arrogant, and deeply committed to building a life together. He fixed things around her home, shared stories about his past, and gradually became an integral part of her world. For a successful real estate professional who had dedicated years to building her career, finding someone who seemed to understand and support her ambitions felt like winning the lottery.

The reality, however, was far more sinister. The man Heather knew as Jace Peretti was actually Jason Owen Donald Porter, a convicted criminal with a documented history of romantic manipulation dating back to the mid-1990s. Porter had perfected the art of assuming false identities, crafting elaborate backstories, and systematically gaining the trust of women across the Greater Toronto Area. Unlike the typical online romance criminals who operate from distant locations and avoid face-to-face contact, Porter's approach was uniquely personal and devastatingly effective. He didn't just steal money; he stole years of his victims' lives, their sense of security, and their ability to trust future relationships.

This book represents more than just the story of one woman's betrayal and subsequent quest for justice. It serves as a comprehensive examination of how modern technology has transformed the landscape of interpersonal relationships, creating new opportunities for both genuine connection and sophisticated manipulation. The rise of dating applications, social media platforms, and digital communication tools has fundamentally altered how we meet, court, and fall in love. While these technologies have brought countless people together in meaningful ways, they have also provided new avenues for those with malicious intent to exploit human vulnerability and emotional need.

Heather Rovet's transformation from victim to investigator illustrates the remarkable resilience of the human spirit when confronted with profound betrayal. Rather than retreating into isolation and shame—responses that many victims of romance crimes experience—Heather channeled her anger and heartbreak into a determined pursuit of truth and accountability. Her journey from successful businesswoman to amateur detective reveals both the inadequacies of existing legal frameworks for addressing romance-related crimes and the extraordinary lengths to which ordinary people will go when seeking justice.

The case also highlights critical gaps in how our society understands and responds to romance fraud. Traditional law enforcement approaches often fall short when dealing with crimes that blur the lines between personal relationships and criminal activity. Prosecutors struggle to build cases when evidence has been deliberately destroyed, victims hesitate to come forward due to embarrassment or self-blame, and the legal system frequently treats these crimes as less serious than other forms of fraud. Jason Porter's ability to operate for years with minimal consequences reflects these systemic failures and underscores the need for more comprehensive approaches to prevention, investigation, and prosecution.

Through extensive research involving court documents, police reports, victim testimonies, and exclusive interviews, this biography reconstructs not only the specific events surrounding the Porter case but also the broader social and technological context that made his crimes possible. We examine the psychological profiles of both perpetrators and victims, the role of digital platforms in facilitating romantic deception, and the evolving legal landscape surrounding online crimes. The narrative draws from multiple perspectives, including law enforcement officials, legal experts, mental health professionals, and most importantly, the women whose lives were forever changed by their encounters with Porter.

The story gained national attention when it became the subject of Prime Video's documentary series "ROMCON: Who the F*** Is Jason Porter?" The documentary's premiere in June 2025 brought renewed focus to issues of online safety, digital literacy, and the need for better protection mechanisms within dating platforms. However, the documentary format, while compelling, necessarily condensed years of complex events into a digestible narrative. This biography aims to provide the comprehensive context and detailed analysis that only a full-length book can offer.

Understanding Jason Porter requires examining the intersection of personal trauma, criminal psychology, and technological opportunity. Born into circumstances marked by instability and loss, Porter's early experiences with abandonment and violence created the foundation for a lifetime of manipulation and deceit. His criminal evolution from petty theft to sophisticated romance fraud reflects both his adaptation to changing technologies and his increasingly sophisticated understanding of human psychology. By the time he encountered Heather Rovet, Porter had refined his methods through years of practice, making him particularly dangerous to someone seeking genuine connection.

The broader implications of this case extend far beyond the specific individuals involved. As society becomes increasingly dependent on digital platforms for social connection, understanding the vulnerabilities inherent in these systems becomes crucial for protecting potential victims. The Porter case serves as a cautionary tale about the importance of digital literacy, the need for robust verification systems on dating platforms, and the value of maintaining healthy skepticism even in the pursuit of love and companionship.

This work also explores the remarkable strength demonstrated by Heather Rovet and other victims who chose to speak publicly about their experiences. Their willingness to share painful personal details serves multiple purposes: it helps other potential victims recognize warning signs, it provides validation for those who have experienced similar betrayals, and it contributes to broader societal conversations about consent, manipulation, and the true cost of romance crimes.

The pages that follow chronicle not just a crime story, but a human story about love, trust, betrayal, and ultimately, redemption. It is a testament to the power of truth-telling in the face of deception, the importance of community support in overcoming trauma, and the possibility of transforming personal pain into societal progress. Through Heather's eyes, we witness both the devastating impact of sophisticated manipulation and the remarkable capacity for healing and growth that defines the human experience.

As we navigate an increasingly complex digital landscape, the lessons embedded in this story become more relevant than ever. The challenge lies not in avoiding technology or retreating from the possibility of connection, but in developing the tools, awareness, and support systems necessary to pursue meaningful relationships while protecting ourselves from those who would exploit our most fundamental human needs.

# Chapter One

## *The Making Of A Monster*

### Born to Lose: The Troubled Childhood of Jason Owen Donald Porter

December 21, 1974, marked the beginning of a life that would eventually touch dozens of victims across Canada, leaving a trail of broken hearts and shattered finances in its wake. Jason Owen Donald Porter entered the world in Kitchener, Ontario, to Christine, a twenty-year-old woman barely out of her teenage years herself. The circumstances surrounding his birth were far from ideal—his mother was young, unprepared for parenthood, and involved with a man whose struggles with alcoholism would cast a dark shadow over Jason's earliest years.

Christine Porter was not equipped for the challenges of raising a child in 1974. The economic landscape of Kitchener during that era was marked by industrial uncertainty, and young families often found themselves struggling to make ends meet. For Christine, who had limited education and few career prospects, the arrival of Jason represented both a blessing and an overwhelming responsibility. The father, whose identity remains somewhat obscured in official records but whose presence was marked by instability and addiction, provided little in the way of emotional or financial support.

The early years of Jason's life were characterized by uncertainty and inconsistency. According to family court documents that would later surface during his adult legal proceedings, Jason's biological father maintained sporadic contact with the family, appearing and disappearing from their lives in patterns that left young Jason confused about male role models and family stability. The alcoholism that plagued his father created an environment where promises were frequently broken, expectations were rarely met, and emotional security was a foreign concept.

In 1978, when Jason was four years old, his world expanded with the arrival of a younger brother. Rather than bringing stability to the household, the addition of another child placed additional strain on an already fragile family structure. Christine found herself responsible for two young children while managing her own emotional and financial struggles. The presence of an alcoholic partner, combined with the demands of caring for two small children, created a powder keg of domestic tension that would eventually explode.

The breaking point came when Jason's biological father's drinking reached crisis levels. Court records from later custody proceedings suggest that domestic violence may have been a factor in Christine's decision to leave, though specific details remain sealed in juvenile protection files. What is clear is that Christine made the difficult decision to remove herself and her children from what had become an untenable situation. This departure, while necessary for their safety, would prove to be the first in a series of abandonments and losses that would fundamentally shape Jason's understanding of relationships and trust.

Following her separation from Jason's biological father, Christine struggled to rebuild her life while caring for two young children. The social safety nets available to single mothers in the late 1970s were limited, and Christine found herself navigating welfare systems, housing instability, and the constant pressure of making ends meet. For Jason, now approaching his fifth birthday, these years were marked by frequent moves, changing caregivers, and an increasing awareness that his family was different from those portrayed in popular culture or observed in more stable households.

It was during this period of upheaval that Christine met Bob, a young radio announcer working in the Kitchener area. Bob represented hope for stability and normalcy that had been absent from Jason's early years. Unlike his biological father, Bob was employed, reliable, and genuinely interested in building a relationship not just with Christine but with her children as well. For the first time in Jason's young life, there was a consistent male presence who attended school events, helped with homework, and provided the kind of steady emotional support that every child needs.

The relationship between Bob and Jason developed gradually but meaningfully. Bob understood that gaining the trust of a child who had already experienced abandonment would require patience and consistency. He made genuine efforts to engage with Jason's interests, supported his academic endeavors, and provided the kind of masculine guidance that had been absent from the boy's early years. For Jason, Bob represented what a father could be—reliable, present, and genuinely caring.

Under Bob's influence, the family began to stabilize. Christine found emotional support and practical assistance that allowed her to focus on creating a more nurturing environment for her children. Jason, now in elementary school, began to show signs of the intelligence and charm that would later become his most dangerous weapons. Teachers noted his quick wit and ability to connect with adults, traits that Bob encouraged through positive reinforcement and genuine interest in Jason's development.

The household during these years represented perhaps the only period of genuine stability and emotional security that Jason would ever experience. Bob's presence brought structure to daily routines, consistency to family expectations, and most importantly, a sense of security that allowed both children to begin developing trust in adult relationships. For Jason, who had spent his earliest years in environments marked by chaos and unpredictability, this stability was transformative.

However, even during these more stable years, observers noted certain troubling characteristics in Jason's behavior. He displayed an unusual ability to manipulate situations to his advantage, often charming adults while simultaneously engaging in behaviors that suggested a lack of empathy for others. Teachers reported incidents where Jason would lie convincingly about completed assignments, blame classmates for his own mistakes, and demonstrate an uncanny ability to avoid consequences through sheer force of personality.

These early manipulative behaviors, while concerning to some educators, were often dismissed as normal childhood testing of boundaries. Bob and Christine, focused on providing stability and positive reinforcement, may have inadvertently enabled some of these behaviors by consistently believing Jason's explanations and failing to implement consistent consequences for dishonesty. The charm that would later become Jason's most effective tool for victimizing women was already being refined through daily interactions with adults who found his personality engaging and convincing.

The social environment of Kitchener during Jason's elementary years provided numerous opportunities for him to observe and learn about human relationships. As Bob's career in radio progressed, the family occasionally attended industry events where Jason was exposed to adults who made their living through communication, persuasion, and public presentation. These experiences may have contributed to Jason's developing understanding of how personality and charm could be weaponized for personal gain.

Despite the stability provided by Bob's presence, Jason continued to struggle with feelings of abandonment related to his biological father's absence. Child psychology experts who have reviewed the case suggest that the early trauma of paternal abandonment, combined with the uncertainty of his earliest years, created deep-seated insecurities that Jason learned to mask through manipulation and control. The fear of being abandoned again may have driven him to develop strategies for maintaining control over relationships, even at a young age.

**Death, Abandonment, and the Birth of a Criminal Mind**

The fragile stability that had characterized Jason's middle childhood was shattered in 1984 when Bob died suddenly at the age of twenty-five. The cause of death, while not extensively documented in publicly available records, appears to have been unexpected and traumatic for the entire family. For Jason, who was only nine years old at the time, Bob's death represented the loss of the only father figure he had ever truly known and trusted.

The impact of Bob's death on Jason cannot be overstated. Child development experts recognize that the loss of a primary attachment figure during middle childhood can have profound and lasting effects on emotional development, particularly in children who have already experienced early trauma. For Jason, who had finally begun to trust in the possibility of stable relationships, Bob's death confirmed his worst fears about the temporary nature of love and security.

Christine's grief following Bob's death was overwhelming and all-consuming. Having lost her partner, her emotional support system, and potentially her primary source of financial stability, she struggled to maintain the household structure that Bob had helped establish. The woman who had worked so hard to provide stability for her children found herself drowning in grief, depression, and practical concerns about their future. For Jason and his younger brother, their mother's emotional unavailability during this critical period represented yet another form of abandonment.

In the aftermath of Bob's death, family dynamics shifted dramatically. Jason, despite being only nine years old, began to assume responsibilities and exhibit behaviors that suggested premature emotional maturity. However, rather than developing healthy coping mechanisms, Jason appears to have learned that emotional manipulation could be an effective tool for getting needs met and maintaining some sense of control in an unpredictable world.

The decision to send Jason to live with his biological father in Toronto following Bob's death would prove to be catastrophic for his development. The man who had been absent during Jason's formative years was now expected to provide guidance and stability for a grieving, traumatized child. The biological father's ongoing struggles with alcoholism had not been resolved during his absence from Jason's life, and his ability to provide appropriate care for a child dealing with complex trauma was severely limited.

Toronto in the mid-1980s was a city in transition, with increasing urbanization creating both opportunities and dangers for young people. For Jason, who had spent his childhood in the smaller community of Kitchener, the move to Toronto represented not just a change of location but a complete disruption of his social support systems, educational continuity, and sense of identity. He was now living with a virtual stranger who happened to share his DNA but had no real understanding of his emotional needs or developmental challenges.

The environment in his biological father's Toronto home was chaotic and unpredictable. Alcoholism had created a household where mood swings, broken promises, and emotional volatility were the norm rather than the exception. For Jason, who was already struggling with grief and abandonment issues, this environment reinforced his growing belief that adults could not be trusted and that emotional connections were sources of pain rather than comfort.

It was during this period that Jason first came into contact with the juvenile justice system. Court records indicate that his initial offenses were relatively minor—credit card theft, small-scale breaking and entering, and automotive theft. However, these crimes represented more than simple adolescent rebellion; they were the first signs of Jason's developing belief that rules applied to other people and that he could manipulate systems to his advantage.

The pattern of criminal behavior that emerged during Jason's teenage years was characterized by escalation and sophistication. What began as impulsive acts of theft evolved into more calculated schemes that demonstrated his growing understanding of human psychology and system vulnerabilities. Youth detention facilities, rather than providing rehabilitation, became educational institutions where Jason learned more advanced criminal techniques and developed relationships with other young offenders.

The summer of 1993 brought the final devastating blow to Jason's already fractured world when Christine died in a car accident. Jason was eighteen years old, legally an adult but emotionally still the traumatized child who had lost Bob nine years earlier. His mother's death eliminated the last potential source of stability and emotional connection in his life, leaving him completely adrift in a world that had repeatedly demonstrated its capacity for sudden and devastating loss.

The inheritance that Jason's younger brother received following Christine's death represented an opportunity for Jason to demonstrate either genuine rehabilitation or continued criminal thinking. His decision to manipulate his brother out of five thousand dollars under the pretense of starting a new life in British Columbia, only to use the money for personal gratification, marked a clear turning point in his criminal evolution. This was no longer a traumatized child acting out; this was a young adult making calculated decisions to exploit family relationships for personal gain.

The psychological foundation for Jason's later crimes against romantic partners was firmly established during these formative years of loss, abandonment, and systematic betrayal of trust. Every significant relationship in his early life had ended in abandonment or death, creating a worldview where emotional connections were temporary at best and exploitative at worst. The charm and intelligence that might have been channeled into positive achievements in different circumstances had been shaped by trauma into tools for manipulation and control.

By the time Jason reached adulthood, the combination of early abandonment, repeated losses, exposure to criminal environments, and lack of positive adult guidance had created someone fundamentally incapable of forming genuine emotional connections. The deaths of Bob and Christine had not inspired him toward positive change, as he would later claim, but had instead confirmed his deepest fears about the nature of human relationships and set him on a path toward viewing other people as resources to be exploited rather than individuals deserving of respect and honesty.

# Chapter Two

## *Apprentice years*

### Juvenile Halls and First Cons: Learning Trade

Ontario's youth detention system in the 1990s was experiencing unprecedented strain as urban crime rates climbed and traditional rehabilitation programs struggled to address increasingly complex cases. Jason Porter entered this system as a fourteen-year-old whose early criminal activities had escalated from impulsive mischief to calculated theft. His first official encounter with juvenile authorities came following a credit card fraud scheme that demonstrated both his natural intelligence and his complete disregard for legal boundaries.

Inside detention facilities across Toronto, Jason discovered a world where cunning and manipulation were valued survival skills rather than character flaws. Fellow inmates, many dealing with their own histories of abandonment and trauma, provided Jason with his first comprehensive education in criminal methodology. However, while other young offenders focused on physical crimes or drug-related activities, Jason gravitated toward schemes that exploited human psychology rather than brute force.

Youth counselors who worked with Jason during his initial detention periods noted his exceptional ability to present himself as reformed and motivated. He participated enthusiastically in group therapy sessions, expressed remorse for his actions with convincing sincerity, and demonstrated what appeared to be genuine insight into his behavioral patterns. These performances were so effective that several counselors recommended early release programs, believing they had witnessed authentic rehabilitation in progress.

Jason's cellmates and fellow detainees became his unwitting professors in an advanced curriculum of deception. From older inmates, he learned how to forge documents with greater sophistication, how to research potential victims through public records, and most importantly, how to identify psychological vulnerabilities that could be exploited. Unlike his peers who often bragged about violent confrontations or drug deals, Jason absorbed lessons about patience, long-term planning, and maintaining multiple false identities simultaneously.

Breaking and entering charges that accumulated during his mid-teens revealed Jason's evolving criminal philosophy. Rather than targeting homes for valuable electronics or jewelry like typical teenage burglars, Jason focused on gathering personal information that could be used for identity theft and financial fraud. He studied family photographs, memorized personal details found in correspondence, and collected documentation that would later enable him to assume aspects of his victims' identities.

During group therapy sessions mandated by court orders, Jason perfected his ability to mirror emotional responses and provide answers that authority figures wanted to hear. Licensed social workers documented his apparent progress in understanding the impact of his crimes on victims, his expressed commitment to making amends, and his articulated plans for building a legitimate future. These reports, filed with juvenile courts, painted a picture of a young man who had learned from his mistakes and was ready to contribute positively to society.

Motor vehicle theft charges added another dimension to Jason's criminal education. While other car thieves focused on joyriding or stripping vehicles for parts, Jason used stolen cars primarily as tools for conducting surveillance on potential future targets. He would observe residential neighborhoods, study family routines, and identify households that might provide opportunities for document theft or financial fraud. His approach to car theft was methodical rather than impulsive, demonstrating an unusual level of strategic thinking for someone his age.

Detention facility staff members, overwhelmed by caseloads and focused on managing immediate behavioral issues, often missed subtle signs of Jason's continued criminal thinking. His ability to maintain perfect institutional behavior while mentally cataloguing information about staff members, their schedules, and facility security procedures demonstrated a level of compartmentalization that would later serve him well in romantic relationships. He learned to present one face to authority figures while maintaining entirely different internal motivations and plans.

Educational programs within juvenile facilities provided Jason with unexpected opportunities to refine his manipulation skills. Computer literacy classes, intended to provide inmates with legitimate job skills, instead taught Jason how to navigate early internet systems and understand digital information storage. These technical skills, combined with his natural talent for deception, would prove invaluable as online communication began revolutionizing how people formed relationships.

Psychological evaluations conducted during Jason's detention periods consistently failed to identify the depth of his antisocial tendencies. His high intelligence and verbal skills enabled him to provide responses that satisfied evaluation criteria while concealing his true thought processes. Mental health professionals noted his traumatic childhood experiences and recommended continued counseling, but they missed underlying patterns of manipulation and emotional emptiness that would define his adult criminal career.

Release and reoffense cycles became Jason's graduate school in criminal methodology. Each return to detention brought new cellmates with different specializations, expanded his knowledge of legal system vulnerabilities, and reinforced his belief that conventional society was populated by naive individuals ripe for exploitation. His growing criminal network provided resources and opportunities that extended far beyond what any single individual could accomplish alone.

Court-mandated community service assignments placed Jason in direct contact with potential future victims while simultaneously burnishing his public image as a reformed young offender. Volunteer work at community centers and charitable organizations provided him with access to personal information about vulnerable individuals while creating positive references that he could cite in future court proceedings. His supervisors consistently praised his reliability, enthusiasm, and genuine concern for others—all carefully constructed performances designed to serve his long-term interests.

## University of Hard Knocks: From Petty Crime to Romance Fraud

Transition from juvenile to adult criminal justice system marked a critical evolution in Jason's criminal methodology. Adult facilities exposed him to more sophisticated criminals whose operations spanned multiple provinces and whose victims numbered in the hundreds. However, rather than joining existing criminal organizations, Jason began developing his own unique approach that combined elements of confidence schemes, identity theft, and psychological manipulation.

Early adult convictions for forgery and possession of stolen property demonstrated Jason's growing sophistication in document manipulation and identity assumption. Unlike crude forgeries typical of street-level criminals, Jason's false documents were meticulously crafted and supported by extensive research into his assumed identities. He studied genuine documents to understand security features, practiced signatures until they became second nature, and developed backstories detailed enough to withstand casual investigation.

Prison educational programs provided Jason with legitimate credentials that enhanced his ability to assume professional identities. He completed computer science coursework, business administration certificates, and communication skills training—all of which served to make his future false personas more believable. Instructors praised his dedication to learning and his apparent commitment to rehabilitation, never suspecting that education was simply another tool in his criminal arsenal.

Fellow inmates introduced Jason to concepts that would later become central to his romance fraud methodology. Confident men serving sentences for investment fraud taught him about building long-term relationships with marks, maintaining multiple false identities simultaneously, and extracting maximum financial benefit from each victim. These conversations, conducted in prison recreation areas and dormitories, provided practical instruction in psychological manipulation techniques that no legitimate educational institution could offer.

Legal research conducted during his incarceration revealed important insights about romance fraud prosecution difficulties. Jason studied case law, sentencing guidelines, and evidence requirements for various types of fraud charges. He learned that romance-related crimes were often difficult to prosecute due to blurred lines between personal relationships and criminal activity, victim reluctance to testify, and challenges in proving criminal intent when genuine emotions appeared to be involved.

Release from adult facilities coincided with explosive growth in internet usage and online dating platforms. Jason immediately recognized that digital communication offered unprecedented opportunities for romantic manipulation. He could maintain relationships with multiple women simultaneously, control information flow more effectively than face-to-face interactions allowed, and establish emotional connections without geographical limitations. Early dating websites became his hunting grounds for identifying potential victims.

False identity creation became Jason's primary criminal focus as he recognized that successful romance fraud required believable personas that could withstand extended scrutiny. He established credit histories for fictional identities, created employment records with companies that could not be easily verified, and developed detailed personal histories complete with childhood memories, family relationships, and life experiences. Each false identity represented months of careful construction and supporting documentation.

University of Waterloo became central to Jason's most effective false persona, despite his never having attended classes there. He studied university catalogs, memorized campus layouts, researched faculty members, and familiarized himself with computer science curriculum details. This knowledge enabled him to convincingly portray himself as a university graduate during conversations with potential romantic partners, lending credibility to his claims of professional success and educational achievement.

Employment history fabrication required Jason to understand various industries well enough to discuss work experiences convincingly. He researched software companies, familiarized himself with technical terminology, and created professional references using accomplices who would vouch for his fictional work history. These elaborate preparations enabled him to maintain consistent stories across multiple relationships and resist attempts by suspicious partners to verify his background.

Financial fraud techniques evolved from simple credit card theft to sophisticated schemes involving bank account manipulation, credit application fraud, and identity assumption for major purchases. Jason learned to exploit weaknesses in financial institution verification procedures, taking advantage of relationship trust to gain access to personal financial information that could be used for fraudulent applications and unauthorized transactions.

Psychological manipulation strategies refined during this period focused specifically on romantic relationships rather than general confidence schemes. Jason studied relationship psychology, learned to identify women seeking stability and emotional connection, and developed techniques for accelerating intimacy while maintaining emotional distance himself. He understood that successful romance fraud required making victims feel special and chosen while gradually normalizing requests for financial assistance or personal information.

Geographic mobility became essential to Jason's criminal methodology as he learned to exploit jurisdictional complications in fraud investigations. Moving between cities and provinces made it difficult for law enforcement agencies to coordinate investigations, enabled him to abandon compromised identities while establishing new ones, and provided access to fresh pools of potential victims who had no knowledge of his criminal history.

Professional counseling and anger management courses, mandated by family court proceedings related to custody disputes, ironically provided Jason with additional insights into human psychology and relationship dynamics. He learned to identify emotional triggers, understand attachment styles, and recognize vulnerability patterns that made certain individuals more susceptible to manipulation. These skills, intended to help him develop healthier relationships, instead became weapons in his arsenal of romantic deception.

By his mid-twenties, Jason had developed criminal methodologies that combined traditional confidence schemes with modern technology and psychological manipulation techniques specifically designed for romantic relationships. His apprentice years had provided him with technical skills, emotional intelligence, and strategic thinking that would enable him to victimize dozens of women across Canada while maintaining freedom for over a decade. Each relationship became both a criminal opportunity and a laboratory for refining his techniques for future victims.

# Chapter Three

## *Digital Romeo*

### Evolution of Online Dating and Perfect Hunting Ground

Internet dating emerged in the late 1990s as a revolutionary solution to urban loneliness and busy professional lifestyles. Match.com launched in 1995, followed by numerous competitors that promised to connect compatible individuals through sophisticated algorithms and detailed personality profiles. For legitimate users, these platforms offered unprecedented access to potential partners beyond geographical and social limitations. For Jason Porter, they represented something far more sinister: a perfect hunting ground where psychological manipulation could flourish behind carefully constructed digital facades.

Traditional dating required face-to-face meetings, shared social circles, and gradual relationship development that made deception difficult to maintain long-term. Online platforms eliminated these natural safeguards, allowing users to control information flow, present idealized versions of themselves, and establish emotional connections before meeting in person. Jason immediately recognized that digital communication offered numerous advantages for someone whose primary skill was psychological manipulation.

Early dating websites like PlentyOfFish, which became operational in 2003, attracted millions of users seeking genuine connections while inadvertently creating fertile ground for romance fraud. These platforms required minimal identity verification, relied primarily on user-submitted information, and provided extensive personal details about potential targets. Members shared relationship histories, financial circumstances, family situations, and emotional vulnerabilities—information that legitimate users viewed as necessary for compatibility assessment but that predators like Jason saw as intelligence gathering opportunities.

Profile creation on multiple platforms became Jason's primary criminal focus as he understood that successful romance fraud required accessing large pools of potential victims. He maintained accounts on numerous dating websites simultaneously, each featuring different versions of his false identity tailored to attract specific demographic groups. Professional women seeking stability, divorced mothers rebuilding their lives, and successful business women looking for intellectual equals all became targets for carefully customized personas.

Messaging systems on dating platforms provided Jason with unprecedented control over relationship pacing and emotional manipulation. Unlike telephone conversations or face-to-face meetings, written communication allowed him to craft responses carefully, research appropriate topics between messages, and maintain consistent lies across multiple relationships. He could express emotions he didn't feel, make promises he never intended to keep, and create intimacy through carefully constructed vulnerability that bore no resemblance to his actual thoughts or feelings.

Geographic flexibility offered by online dating enabled Jason to pursue victims across vast distances while maintaining multiple relationships simultaneously. Women in Vancouver, Toronto, Montreal, and other major Canadian cities became potential targets regardless of where Jason happened to be physically located. This geographic spread made it difficult for victims to compare experiences, reduced chances of discovery through mutual acquaintances, and complicated law enforcement investigations when crimes were eventually reported.

Technological advancement in digital photography and image manipulation provided Jason with tools for creating convincing visual representations of his false identities. He learned to select photographs that suggested success and stability without being easily traceable through reverse image searches. Professional headshots, casual lifestyle images, and carefully staged photographs supported his fictional narratives while maintaining enough authenticity to withstand casual scrutiny from romantically interested women.

Privacy settings and communication controls on dating platforms allowed Jason to manage information flow and prevent victims from accessing details that might contradict his constructed identity. He could limit photograph visibility, control profile information access, and terminate conversations instantly if questions became too probing or verification attempts seemed likely. These digital tools provided escape mechanisms that traditional dating scenarios would never have offered.

Search algorithms used by dating websites inadvertently assisted Jason's targeting strategies by identifying women whose profiles indicated vulnerability factors that made them susceptible to romance fraud. Divorced women, single mothers, professionals focused on career advancement, and individuals explicitly seeking long-term commitment became his preferred targets because their profiles suggested emotional needs that could be exploited through sustained manipulation.

Communication patterns on dating platforms revealed important intelligence about potential victims before Jason invested significant time in relationship development. Women who responded quickly to messages, shared personal information readily, and expressed enthusiasm for meeting someone special demonstrated characteristics that suggested they might be susceptible to accelerated intimacy and emotional manipulation. Jason learned to identify these patterns and prioritize relationships accordingly.

Online safety education during the early internet dating era was minimal and often focused on physical meeting safety rather than sophisticated psychological manipulation. Most dating safety advice emphasized meeting in public places and informing friends about dates, but provided little guidance about identifying emotional predators or recognizing signs of financial fraud. This educational gap left users vulnerable to exactly the type of sophisticated manipulation that Jason had perfected.

Dating platform business models inadvertently supported Jason's criminal activities by prioritizing user engagement over identity verification. Subscription-based websites wanted members to remain active and communicative, creating environments where extended online relationships were encouraged rather than scrutinized. Success stories featured couples who had corresponded for months before meeting, normalizing patterns that also characterized predatory behavior.

**Crafting Perfect Persona: How Jason Became "Jace Peretti"**

Creating "Jace Peretti" required months of careful planning and detailed construction that went far beyond simple name changes or fictional employment history. Jason understood that successful long-term deception needed a persona so thoroughly developed that he could inhabit it completely, responding to unexpected questions spontaneously while maintaining consistency across all interactions. Jace Peretti became Jason's masterpiece of identity manipulation, combining enough truth to feel authentic with enough fiction to serve his criminal purposes.

Personality development for Jace Peretti began with Jason studying successful men who attracted women through combinations of professional achievement, emotional availability, and masculine competence. He researched communication styles, relationship approaches, and behavioral patterns that appealed to his target demographic of educated, successful women seeking stable partnerships. Jace became everything that Jason understood these women desired in a romantic partner.

Physical appearance aspects of Jace Peretti identity required Jason to modify his actual appearance in ways that supported his fictional narrative while remaining sustainable long-term. He improved his physical fitness, upgraded his wardrobe to suggest professional success, and developed grooming habits that reinforced his claims of software engineering career and upper-middle-class lifestyle. These changes served dual purposes of supporting his false identity and making him more appealing to potential victims.

Professional background construction formed the cornerstone of Jace Peretti's believability because employment history provided explanations for financial resources, lifestyle choices, and scheduling flexibility that romance fraud required. Jason's fictional software engineering career at University of Waterloo provided explanations for technical knowledge, international travel, and irregular schedules that accommodated multiple relationships. He memorized computer science terminology, studied industry trends, and developed convincing explanations for work-related absences.

Family history creation for Jace Peretti balanced generating sympathy and emotional connection

52

while avoiding details that could be easily verified or contradicted. Jason constructed a background featuring deceased parents, limited family connections, and childhood experiences that explained both his emotional availability and his independence from family scrutiny. This fictional history generated empathy from victims while eliminating people who might contradict his stories or interfere with his criminal activities.

Geographic background establishment required Jason to become intimately familiar with locations where Jace Peretti supposedly lived and worked. He studied neighborhood characteristics, local businesses, school systems, and cultural landmarks that would enable him to discuss these areas convincingly during conversations with potential victims. This research allowed him to answer unexpected questions spontaneously while maintaining the illusion of genuine personal history.

Hobby and interest development for Jace Peretti involved Jason acquiring superficial knowledge about activities that attracted his target demographic while avoiding commitments that might interfere with his criminal operations. He learned enough about wine, travel, literature, and cultural activities to engage in sophisticated conversations while avoiding deep expertise that might be tested through extended interaction. These interests made Jace appear well-rounded and culturally sophisticated.

Emotional availability became Jace Peretti's most powerful attraction factor because Jason understood that his target victims were seeking genuine emotional connection rather than casual relationships. He studied relationship psychology, learned to mirror emotional expressions, and developed techniques for creating rapid intimacy through carefully orchestrated vulnerability. Jace appeared emotionally mature, communicative, and ready for serious commitment—qualities that made him irresistible to women seeking stable partnerships.

Communication style development required Jason to modify his natural speech patterns, vocabulary choices, and interaction approaches to match Jace Peretti's fictional background and personality. He practiced expressing emotions he didn't feel, developed comfort with romantic language, and learned to ask questions that demonstrated genuine interest while actually gathering intelligence for future manipulation. This communication transformation was so complete that many victims later described feeling as though they had met two completely different people.

Documentation creation for Jace Peretti identity involved producing physical evidence that supported his fictional narrative without creating legal vulnerabilities or verification risks. Jason developed business cards, created social media profiles with appropriate history, and generated documentation that suggested legitimate employment and lifestyle without directly impersonating specific individuals or companies. This supporting evidence made Jace Peretti seem genuine during casual scrutiny.

Behavioral consistency training required Jason to practice inhabiting Jace Peretti's personality so completely that responses became automatic rather than calculated. He developed muscle memory for Jace's mannerisms, practiced emotional responses until they appeared genuine, and learned to maintain character even during unexpected situations or stressful confrontations. This level of preparation enabled him to sustain deception for years rather than weeks or months.

Vulnerability scripting involved Jason creating carefully planned revelations about Jace Peretti's supposed fears, insecurities, and emotional needs that would generate protective instincts and deeper emotional attachment from victims. These manufactured vulnerabilities were designed to accelerate intimacy while creating obligations that victims felt compelled to fulfill through emotional support, financial assistance, or personal sacrifice. Each revelation was calculated to deepen emotional investment while advancing Jason's criminal objectives.

# Chapter Four

## *Heather Rovet Story*

### Success in Six: A Real Estate Powerhouse's Rise

Heather Rovet built her real estate empire through relentless dedication, exceptional market knowledge, and an intuitive understanding of what clients needed most during one of life's biggest decisions. By 2018, she had established herself as one of Toronto's most respected luxury real estate professionals, specializing in helping successful individuals find homes that matched both their financial capabilities and their lifestyle aspirations. Her tagline, "Helping people find their perfect home or condo for the Next Chapter of their Life," reflected not just her business philosophy but her genuine commitment to understanding clients as complete human beings rather than simple transactions.

Toronto's competitive real estate market demanded professionals who could navigate complex negotiations, understand neighborhood dynamics, and build trust with clients making million-dollar decisions. Heather excelled in all these areas, but her greatest strength lay in her ability to listen carefully to what clients expressed directly while also understanding their unspoken concerns and desires. She possessed an emotional intelligence that enabled her to guide nervous first-time buyers, reassure downsizing empty nesters, and counsel ambitious professionals seeking investment properties.

Professional success in Toronto real estate required working with diverse clientele ranging from young professionals purchasing their first condominiums to established families seeking luxury homes in prestigious neighborhoods. Heather developed expertise across multiple market segments, understanding everything from downtown condo developments to suburban family neighborhoods to exclusive Rosedale properties. This broad knowledge base made her valuable to clients and referral sources while establishing her reputation as someone who could handle any real estate challenge.

Building her business demanded significant personal sacrifices that many successful professionals understand intimately. Weekends were consumed by property showings, evenings were dedicated to client consultations, and vacations were frequently interrupted by urgent client needs. Heather's commitment to excellence meant that personal relationships often took secondary priority to professional obligations, a common pattern among driven individuals who achieve significant career success at the expense of work-life balance.

Financial independence through real estate success provided Heather with security and lifestyle options that many women her age envied. She owned her midtown Toronto condominium outright, maintained healthy investment portfolios, and enjoyed the freedom that comes with professional achievement and financial stability. However, material success has not filled the emotional void that many successful professionals experience when career achievement fails to provide complete life satisfaction.

Social circles surrounding Toronto's real estate industry included other professionals, successful clients, and business contacts who shared similar achievement-oriented lifestyles. While these relationships provided networking opportunities and professional support, they often lacked the emotional depth and genuine intimacy that Heather increasingly craved as she reached her forties. Professional success had brought many rewards, but romantic fulfillment remained elusive despite her accomplishments in other life areas.

Dating challenges for successful professional women in major cities are well-documented sociological phenomena that reflect broader cultural tensions about gender roles, professional achievement, and relationship dynamics. Men often felt intimidated by Heather's success, while others seemed more interested in her financial stability than her personal qualities. Finding someone who appreciated her achievements without feeling threatened by them proved surprisingly difficult in a city filled with ambitious professionals.

Personal growth through professional success had taught Heather valuable lessons about persistence, integrity, and building trust with strangers. She understood how to read people's motivations, identify their needs, and develop relationships based on mutual benefit and genuine care. These skills, which served her exceptionally well in real estate, would ironically make her more vulnerable to someone who understood how to exploit empathy and trust for malicious purposes.

Community involvement became increasingly important to Heather as her business matured and she sought ways to use her success for positive impact beyond individual transactions. She supported local charities, mentored young women entering real estate careers, and participated in community development initiatives that improved neighborhoods where she worked. This civic engagement reflected her fundamental belief in contributing to something larger than personal achievement.

Lifestyle management for successful real estate professionals requires careful attention to personal presentation, home environment, and social connections that support both business development and personal satisfaction. Heather maintained her condominium as both a personal sanctuary and a showcase of her aesthetic sensibilities, understanding that clients often judged professional competence based on how successfully agents managed their own living situations.

Professional networking within Toronto's real estate community provided Heather with ongoing education, business opportunities, and peer support from others who understood the unique demands of high-end property sales. Industry conferences, professional association meetings, and informal gatherings with colleagues created a social framework that supported her business while providing limited opportunities for the deeper personal connections she increasingly desired.

Work-life balance remained an ongoing challenge as Heather's success demanded increasing time commitments while her personal life remained unfulfilled. Friends encouraged her to try online dating, take vacations, and prioritize personal relationships, but the demanding nature of real estate sales made it difficult to maintain consistent availability for relationship development. This tension between professional demands and personal needs created vulnerability that would later be exploited by someone who understood exactly how to position himself as a solution to her dilemma.

**Knock at Door: When Love Walked In**

July 9, 2018, began as an ordinary summer Monday in Heather's well-organized life. Her midtown Toronto condominium required minor kitchen cabinet repairs, and she had arranged for a handyman through a renovation company she had used previously. Based on past experience, she expected to see a familiar face—an older, heavyset gentleman who had completed similar work competently if unremarkably. Heather planned to let him in, show him the problem, and continue with her morning routine while he worked.

Morning sunlight streamed through her condo windows as Heather prepared for another busy day of client meetings and property showings. Her professional wardrobe was selected, coffee was brewing, and she was mentally reviewing her schedule when the anticipated knock came at her door. Opening it without hesitation, expecting to greet a familiar tradesman, Heather instead found herself looking at someone completely unexpected.

Standing in her doorway was a man in his forties whose presence immediately commanded attention. Salt-and-pepper hair suggested maturity and experience, while his genuine smile featured a charming gap between his front teeth that somehow made him seem both sophisticated and approachable. His overall appearance suggested someone who took care of himself physically while maintaining the kind of unpretentious confidence that comes from genuine competence rather than manufactured bravado.

Introduction came with a warm handshake and direct eye contact as he identified himself as Jace Peretti. His voice carried just enough authority to suggest professional competence while remaining warm enough to put her at ease. Unlike the minimal interaction she typically had with service providers, Jace's manner invited conversation and suggested someone who viewed each job as an opportunity for genuine human connection rather than just another task to complete efficiently.

Professional competence became immediately apparent as Jace examined her kitchen cabinets and explained the repair process in terms that demonstrated both technical knowledge and respect for her intelligence. He didn't talk down to her or assume she lacked understanding of basic home maintenance, but neither did he overwhelm her with unnecessary technical details. His approach suggested someone who had worked with educated, successful clients and understood how to communicate appropriately.

Conversation flowed naturally as Jace worked, covering topics that revealed shared interests and compatible worldviews. He mentioned his son, his previous career in software engineering, and his decision to work with his hands rather than spending all day behind a computer. These details painted a picture of someone who had made thoughtful life choices, valued work-life balance, and prioritized personal satisfaction over purely financial considerations.

Unexpected chemistry developed as their conversation continued beyond the basic politeness typically exchanged between homeowners and service providers. Jace asked thoughtful questions about her neighborhood, expressed genuine interest in her observations about Toronto's real estate market, and shared perspectives that suggested both intelligence and emotional maturity. For someone whose professional life involved constant interaction with people, finding someone who could engage her intellectually while maintaining appropriate boundaries felt refreshing.

Time seemed to pass more quickly than usual as Jace completed his cabinet repairs and Heather found herself reluctant to see him leave. When she mentioned needing towel bars installed in her bathrooms, his immediate willingness to help suggested someone who genuinely enjoyed both the work and the opportunity to continue their conversation. This extension of his visit felt natural rather than forced, creating the impression that he, too, was enjoying their interaction.

Extended interaction during bathroom fixture installation provided more opportunities for meaningful conversation and mutual assessment. Jace shared stories about his past that revealed resilience, integrity, and the kind of life experiences that create depth and character. His comments about balancing career success with personal fulfillment resonated with Heather's own struggles to maintain perspective amid professional demands.

Professional boundary dissolution happened so gradually that Heather barely noticed the transition from service provider relationship to personal connection. Jace's combination of competence, respectfulness, and genuine interest in her as a person created the foundation for something that felt like the beginning of a meaningful relationship. His presence filled her home with an energy that had been missing, and his departure left her looking forward to seeing him again.

Future possibilities seemed to open naturally as their day together concluded. Rather than simply completing his work and leaving, Jace expressed interest in seeing her again outside of any professional context. His approach was confident without being presumptuous, suggesting someone who understood how to express romantic interest while respecting boundaries and allowing her to respond authentically to the attraction that had developed between them.

Reflection after Jace's departure left Heather feeling hopeful about possibilities she hadn't seriously considered in years. Professional success had provided many satisfactions, but meeting someone who seemed to appreciate both her achievements and her personal qualities suggested that the life balance she had been seeking might finally be within reach. The handyman who had knocked on her door that morning had introduced possibilities that extended far beyond cabinet repairs and bathroom fixtures.

# Chapter Five

## *Three Years Of Lies*

**Building Perfect Relationship: Art of Long-Term Deception**

Jace Peretti's courtship of Heather Rovet unfolded with remarkable precision, demonstrating sophisticated understanding of relationship psychology and emotional manipulation that had been refined through years of practice. Unlike impulsive criminals who seek immediate gratification, Jason Porter understood that sustained deception required patience, consistency, and genuine investment in creating experiences that felt authentic to his victim. Over three years, he constructed what appeared to be a loving partnership while systematically exploiting Heather's trust for his own purposes.

Initial relationship development proceeded at a pace that felt natural and comfortable to Heather while serving Jason's strategic objectives. He balanced attentiveness with independence, demonstrating interest without appearing desperate or overly eager. Follow-up contact after their first meeting came at appropriate intervals, suggesting someone who was genuinely interested but respectful of boundaries. This careful pacing created anticipation and emotional investment while avoiding behaviors that might trigger suspicion or resistance.

Emotional intimacy acceleration required Jason to share carefully crafted vulnerabilities that would generate protective instincts and deeper attachment from Heather. He revealed supposed fears, disappointments, and personal struggles that painted him as emotionally available and trustworthy while creating opportunities for Heather to provide comfort and support. These manufactured revelations served dual purposes of deepening her emotional investment while establishing patterns where she felt responsible for his well being.

Consistency maintenance across multiple aspects of their relationship demanded exceptional attention to detail and remarkable memory for previously shared information. Jason maintained detailed mental records of stories he had told, promises he had made, and personal details he had shared to avoid contradictions that might expose his deception. This level of preparation enabled him to respond spontaneously to unexpected questions while maintaining the illusion of genuine personal history and authentic emotional connection.

Living situation integration happened gradually as Jason spent increasing amounts of time at Heather's condominium, contributing to household expenses and maintenance in ways that suggested genuine partnership rather than exploitation. He performed repairs, contributed to groceries, and participated in domestic responsibilities that made him seem like a committed partner rather than someone seeking financial advantage. This domestic integration made their relationship feel established and permanent while providing him with ongoing access to her personal information and financial resources.

Social circle introduction required Jason to present himself convincingly to Heather's friends, family members, and professional colleagues who might scrutinize his background or question his intentions. He researched her social connections through social media and casual conversation, preparing appropriate responses to likely questions while avoiding situations that might expose inconsistencies in his fabricated identity. His charm and apparent sincerity convinced most observers that Heather had found a genuinely caring partner.

Professional identity maintenance involved Jason continuing to present himself as a successful software engineer while managing the practical challenges of maintaining this fiction during an extended relationship. He created plausible explanations for work schedules, travel requirements, and client meetings that justified his availability for relationship activities while avoiding situations that might require verification of his supposed employment. This balancing act required constant attention to scheduling and careful management of external commitments.

Financial boundary establishment happened so gradually that Heather barely noticed the progression from complete independence to shared expenses and joint financial responsibilities. Jason began by contributing appropriately to shared activities and household expenses, establishing himself as someone who paid his fair share and respected financial boundaries. Over time, he introduced requests for temporary assistance with supposedly short-term financial challenges that would be quickly resolved through his work income.

Gift-giving strategies demonstrated Jason's understanding that successful manipulation required genuine investment in creating positive experiences and emotional memories. He purchased thoughtful presents, planned special occasions, and created romantic gestures that made Heather feel valued and cherished. These investments served multiple purposes of reinforcing her emotional attachment while demonstrating apparent financial stability and genuine affection for her personal happiness.

Family dynamics navigation required Jason to develop convincing explanations for his limited family connections while avoiding situations that might expose contradictions in his background story. He created plausible reasons for maintaining distance from supposed relatives while encouraging Heather's family relationships and demonstrating interest in becoming part of her extended family structure. This approach generated sympathy for his supposed isolation while positioning himself as someone seeking genuine family connection.

Future planning discussions enabled Jason to maintain Heather's long-term commitment while avoiding specific commitments that might expose his deception or interfere with his criminal activities. He engaged enthusiastically in conversations about travel plans, home improvements, and relationship milestones while maintaining enough flexibility to modify or abandon plans when circumstances required. These discussions reinforced Heather's belief in their shared future while serving Jason's need for ongoing access to her resources.

## Red Flags in Paradise: Signs That Were Missed

Communication patterns throughout their relationship contained subtle inconsistencies that might have revealed Jason's deception to someone specifically looking for warning signs. His responses to unexpected questions sometimes came with brief delays that suggested mental calculation rather than spontaneous recall of genuine memories. Phone conversations occasionally featured background noises that didn't match his claimed locations or activities, and his explanations for communication gaps sometimes contained minor contradictions when compared to previous statements.

Work schedule irregularities presented ongoing challenges for Jason that required increasingly creative explanations as their relationship progressed. His supposed software engineering career provided convenient excuses for unpredictable hours, travel requirements, and client emergencies, but careful analysis would have revealed patterns that didn't align with typical technology industry employment. Weekend work that prevented social commitments, emergency travel that couldn't be verified, and project deadlines that conveniently coincided with relationship conflicts might have raised suspicions in different circumstances.

Financial behavior anomalies became more apparent over time as Jason's requests for assistance increased while his contributions to shared expenses became more irregular. His explanations for temporary cash flow problems always included convincing reasons and promised quick resolution, but pattern analysis would have shown recurring cycles of financial difficulty followed by mysterious income sources. Credit card usage patterns, reluctance to discuss specific work projects, and vague responses about banking relationships all represented potential warning signs.

Personal history verification proved impossible whenever Heather showed interest in learning more about Jason's background, family, or past experiences. His childhood stories, while emotionally compelling, lacked specific details that could be confirmed through external sources. Friends from his past were always conveniently unavailable, work colleagues were bound by confidentiality agreements, and family members were estranged for tragic but unverifiable reasons. These barriers to verification created isolation that prevented outside perspective on their relationship.

Social media presence limitations should have raised questions about someone supposedly employed in the technology industry where online professional presence was virtually mandatory.

Jason's minimal digital footprint, reluctance to appear in photographs posted online, and careful management of his social media connections all served his need to maintain multiple identities while avoiding detection. His explanations about privacy concerns and professional requirements for digital discretion were plausible but inconsistent with normal technology worker behavior.

Documentation availability became increasingly problematic when practical relationship needs required official verification of Jason's identity or employment status. Application processes for shared credit accounts, lease agreements, or travel arrangements revealed his reluctance to provide standard documentation or his tendency to create delays until alternative arrangements could be made. These patterns, while individually explainable, collectively suggested someone managing complex deception rather than normal administrative preferences.

Physical evidence inconsistencies accumulated over three years as Jason's presence in Heather's life required increasing integration with her established routines and social connections. Personal belongings that suggested a different lifestyle than his claimed professional status, knowledge gaps about supposed areas of expertise, and behavioral patterns that contradicted his stated values all represented potential indicators of deception. However, these signs were subtle enough to be explained by individual quirks rather than systematic fraud.

Emotional manipulation techniques became more apparent in retrospect as Jason's responses to relationship conflicts followed predictable patterns designed to maintain control while avoiding genuine resolution. His ability to deflect serious conversations, redirect blame, and generate sympathy during confrontations all served to maintain his position while preventing Heather from pursuing uncomfortable questions. These psychological tactics were sophisticated enough to feel like normal relationship dynamics rather than calculated manipulation.

External perspective limitations resulted from Jason's gradual isolation of Heather from friends and family members who might have provided objective assessment of their relationship. This isolation happened so subtly that it felt like natural relationship progression rather than deliberate manipulation, but it effectively removed potential sources of reality-checking that might have exposed inconsistencies in Jason's stories or behavior patterns.

Instinctual warning signals that Heather occasionally experienced were consistently explained away through Jason's charm, apparent vulnerability, and ability to provide plausible explanations for concerning behaviors. Her professional success in reading people made her confident in her judgment, but it also made her susceptible to someone who understood exactly how to exploit that confidence while maintaining just enough authenticity to prevent deeper investigation of troubling patterns.

# Chapter six

## *Unraveling*

### Friend's Discovery: Bumble Photos That Changed Everything

May 2020 arrived with spring optimism that masked underlying tensions threatening to destroy everything Heather believed about her relationship with Jace. After nearly two years together, their partnership seemed stronger than ever, having weathered early pandemic restrictions and emerging with deeper intimacy and shared commitment. Heather had begun imagining their future together with increasing confidence, discussing plans for travel, home improvements, and perhaps even marriage. Nothing in their daily interactions suggested that her world was about to collapse through a casual discovery made by someone whose loyalty would prove more valuable than gold.

Sarah, one of Heather's closest friends and confidantes, had been navigating her own romantic challenges through online dating applications with varying degrees of success and frustration. Like many single women in Toronto, she relied on platforms like Bumble to meet potential partners while maintaining healthy skepticism about profile authenticity and user intentions. Her experience with digital dating had taught her to scrutinize photographs carefully, cross-reference information, and trust instincts when something seemed inconsistent or too good to be true.

Scrolling through potential matches during a quiet evening at home, Sarah encountered a profile that made her freeze with recognition and growing alarm. Photographs that were unmistakably of Jace Peretti appeared under a completely different name, accompanied by personal details that contradicted everything she knew about Heather's boyfriend. Age information didn't match, professional background was entirely different, and relationship history contained discrepancies that suggested either mistaken identity or deliberate deception on a massive scale.

Initial disbelief gave way to careful investigation as Sarah screenshotted the profile and began comparing details with her knowledge of Jace's supposed background. She remembered conversations where Heather had shared information about his career, family history, and personal interests, none of which aligned with the dating profile she had discovered. Professional instincts developed through years of business experience told her that these discrepancies were too significant to be explained by simple mistakes or profile theft.

Decision-making about whether to confront Heather with this discovery required careful consideration of friendship dynamics and potential consequences. Sarah understood that sharing this information would devastate her friend while potentially destroying a relationship that Heather cherished deeply. However, her loyalty to Heather and concern for her wellbeing ultimately outweighed any hesitation about causing immediate pain through unwelcome revelations about someone Heather loved and trusted completely.

Approach strategies for sharing this disturbing discovery required sensitivity and careful timing that would allow Heather to process the information without feeling attacked or defensive. Sarah chose to present the evidence factually while expressing concern and support rather than making accusations or demanding immediate action. She understood that Heather would need time to absorb this information and decide how to respond without pressure from outside sources who might not understand the complexity of her situation.

Heather's initial reaction combined disbelief, defensive loyalty, and rational explanations that could account for the discrepancies without assuming malicious intent. She suggested that someone might have stolen Jace's photographs for their own dating profile, a common occurrence in online dating that could explain the appearance of his images under a different name. This explanation felt more comfortable than considering that her partner of two years had been living a completely fabricated identity while sharing her bed and her life.

Persistence from Sarah, motivated by genuine concern rather than desire to create drama, led to deeper investigation of the dating profile and cross-referencing of information that became increasingly difficult to explain through innocent mistakes. Detailed comparison of supposed personal history, professional background, and family circumstances revealed patterns of deception that extended far beyond simple photograph theft or profile errors. Each new discrepancy made innocent explanations less plausible while pointing toward systematic fraud.

Evidence accumulation became impossible to ignore as Sarah continued researching the dating profile and associated information that painted a picture completely different from the man Heather knew as Jace Peretti. Public records searches, social media investigations, and careful analysis of available information began revealing a web of deception that extended far beyond simple dating profile inconsistencies. This growing evidence demanded explanations that Jace would find difficult to provide without revealing his true identity and criminal history.

Emotional preparation for confronting Jace required Heather to steel herself for conversations that might destroy everything she believed about their relationship while potentially confirming her worst fears about being deceived and manipulated. She wrestled with hoping for innocent explanations while simultaneously preparing for the possibility that someone she loved completely had been systematically exploiting her trust, emotions, and potentially her financial resources for purposes she couldn't yet comprehend.

**Google Search of Horror: When Truth Shattered Reality**

Legal documents discovered during Sarah's investigation contained the name "Jason Porter" in connection with family court proceedings that supposedly involved Jace's custody arrangements with his ex-girlfriend. Initially, this name appeared to support Jace's previous explanations about using pseudonyms for legal protection during his corporate career, providing seemingly innocent reasons for documentation bearing different names. However, these same documents revealed inconsistencies about the number of children involved that contradicted specific information Jace had shared about his family situation.

Curiosity about these discrepancies led Heather to conduct her own internet search for "Jason Porter," expecting to find limited information that would either confirm Jace's explanations or reveal minor inconsistencies that could be easily explained. Instead, her search results opened a window into a criminal history spanning over a decade that left her staring at her computer screen in shocked disbelief while her understanding of reality crumbled around her like a house of cards in an earthquake.

Search results revealed newspaper articles, court documents, and police reports documenting the criminal activities of someone identified as Jason Porter, described by media outlets as a romance scammer who had victimized multiple women across Toronto through sophisticated deception and financial fraud. Headlines described someone dubbed "Online Romeo" whose methods and criminal history bore uncomfortable similarities to behaviors and patterns that Heather now recognized from her own relationship experience.

Photographic evidence provided the final, devastating confirmation that her beloved Jace Peretti and the criminal Jason Porter were the same person. Mugshots and court photographs showed unmistakable facial features, including the distinctive gap-toothed smile that had initially charmed her when he appeared at her door two years earlier. Comparing these official photographs with personal images she had taken during romantic moments revealed the terrible truth that she had been living with and loving someone whose entire identity was a carefully constructed lie.

Emotional devastation hit Heather in waves as she processed the implications of her discovery while scrolling through article after article documenting Jason's criminal activities, previous victims, and court proceedings that painted a picture of someone who had made victimizing women his primary criminal enterprise. Each new detail felt like a physical blow as she realized that moments she had treasured as genuine intimacy had been calculated performances designed to facilitate her exploitation.

Timeline reconstruction became an obsessive necessity as Heather attempted to understand how extensively she had been deceived and whether any aspect of their relationship had been authentic. She mentally reviewed three years of shared experiences, searching for clues she had missed while simultaneously grieving the loss of memories that had once brought her joy but now felt contaminated by knowledge of their fraudulent foundation.

Financial assessment required Heather to examine bank statements, credit card records, and financial transactions to determine the extent of any theft or fraud that might have occurred during their relationship. While Jason had been relatively subtle in his financial exploitation compared to his treatment of previous victims, careful analysis revealed patterns of manipulation and unauthorized access that represented significant financial impact beyond the emotional devastation of romantic betrayal.

Safety concerns became paramount as Heather realized she was sharing living space with someone whose criminal history included multiple victims and whose reaction to discovery remained unpredictable. She faced the terrifying reality that confronting Jason about his true identity might provoke desperate responses from someone who had successfully evaded consequences for his crimes through years of careful deception and manipulation.

Reality acceptance required Heather to acknowledge that everything she believed about her relationship, her judgment, and her ability to trust her own instincts had been systematically undermined by someone whose criminal expertise exceeded her ability to detect deception. This recognition challenged her self-concept as a successful professional who prided herself on reading people accurately and making sound decisions about personal relationships.

Future planning suddenly shifted from romantic dreams to practical concerns about legal protection, financial security, and emotional recovery from trauma that extended far beyond typical relationship dissolution. Heather faced the daunting prospect of rebuilding her life while processing the psychological impact of discovering that someone she had loved completely had viewed her primarily as a criminal opportunity rather than a genuine partner deserving of honesty and respect.

# Chapter seven

## *The Victim Network*

### Sarah's Story: First Known Victim Speaks

Sarah's encounter with Jason Porter began in November 2010 on PlentyOfFish, one of Canada's most popular free dating platforms that promised genuine connections for millions of users seeking love and companionship. As a professional woman in her thirties navigating Toronto's competitive dating scene, Sarah approached online relationships with cautious optimism, understanding that digital platforms offered both opportunities and risks that required careful evaluation and healthy skepticism about potential partners' authenticity and intentions.

Initial contact through PlentyOfFish messaging demonstrated Jason's evolving skill at creating compelling first impressions that balanced confidence with vulnerability, suggesting someone genuinely interested in meaningful connection rather than casual encounters. His messages referenced specific details from Sarah's profile, asked thoughtful questions about her interests and career, and revealed personal information that painted him as an educated, successful professional seeking partnership with someone who shared his values and life goals.

Geographic connections became a powerful tool for establishing credibility as Jason demonstrated intimate knowledge of Sarah's hometown, including elementary schools, local businesses, and community landmarks that suggested genuine familiarity rather than research-based preparation. He claimed to have met her briefly during their university years, providing plausible explanations for his detailed knowledge while creating a sense of destiny and shared history that made their connection feel significant rather than random.

Professional presentation during their first date in Toronto's upscale Yorkville neighborhood showcased Jason's ability to project success and stability through careful attention to appearance, venue selection, and conversation topics that reinforced his claims of international business travel and software engineering expertise. His knowledge of technical terminology, industry trends, and global business practices convinced Sarah that she was meeting someone whose professional achievements matched her own ambitions and standards.

Social integration proceeded rapidly as Jason expressed genuine interest in Sarah's social circle while introducing her to supposed friends and colleagues who supported his fabricated identity. He attended gatherings with her friends, participated in professional networking events, and demonstrated the kind of social skills that suggested someone comfortable in various environments and genuinely interested in building connections beyond their romantic relationship.

Family introduction represented a significant milestone that Jason managed successfully by charming Sarah's parents during holiday visits while gathering crucial personal information that would later facilitate financial fraud. His respectful manner, appropriate gift-giving, and genuine interest in family dynamics convinced Sarah's relatives that she had found someone worthy of their daughter's affection and capable of providing the stability and partnership they wanted for her.

Facebook friendship and social media integration provided Jason with ongoing access to Sarah's personal information, daily activities, and social connections while creating digital evidence of their relationship that supported the illusion of genuine partnership. His careful management of online presence, appropriate commenting on posts, and integration with her digital social life reinforced the authenticity of their connection while providing intelligence for future manipulation.

Financial exploitation began subtly through shared expenses and joint activities that established patterns of reciprocity and mutual support before escalating to more significant requests for assistance with temporary cash flow problems that always included convincing explanations and promises of quick repayment. Jason's approach was sophisticated enough to avoid triggering immediate suspicion while systematically accessing Sarah's financial resources through various mechanisms.

Travel planning for their supposed romantic getaway to Paris and Africa represented the culmination of Jason's manipulation, involving detailed itinerary development, apparent ticket purchases, and elaborate stories about meeting his relatives abroad that generated excitement and emotional investment while serving as cover for more extensive financial fraud involving both Sarah's and her father's credit card information gathered during family visits.

Disappearance in February 2011 came suddenly and completely, leaving Sarah with cancelled travel plans, fraudulent charges, forged airline tickets, and the devastating realization that someone she had loved and trusted for three months had systematically exploited her emotions, finances, and family relationships for criminal purposes. His vanishing act coincided with her discovery of financial irregularities that revealed the true extent of his criminal activities.

Legal reporting to police provided Sarah with her first understanding that Jason Porter was already known to law enforcement and had been recently released from jail for vehicle theft involving another girlfriend he had met through PlentyOfFish. This revelation transformed her understanding of their relationship from romantic disappointment to criminal victimization while highlighting systemic failures that allowed serial predators to continue operating with minimal consequences.

**Web of Broken Hearts: Connecting Dots Across Toronto**

Pattern recognition across multiple victims revealed Jason Porter's systematic approach to romance fraud that involved targeting specific demographic groups, utilizing consistent deception techniques, and exploiting predictable vulnerabilities that made educated, successful women particularly susceptible to his manipulation. Each relationship followed similar developmental patterns while incorporating lessons learned from previous victims to refine his methodology and avoid detection mechanisms that might expose his criminal activities.

Victim demographics showed Jason's preference for financially stable, emotionally available women in their thirties and forties who were seeking serious relationships rather than casual encounters. Professional women, recently divorced individuals, and single mothers represented his primary targets because their profiles indicated both financial resources and emotional needs that could be exploited through sustained manipulation and false promises of partnership and stability.

Geographic distribution of known victims across the Greater Toronto Area demonstrated Jason's strategic use of urban anonymity and transportation networks to maintain multiple relationships simultaneously while avoiding detection through mutual acquaintances or overlapping social circles. His knowledge of various neighborhoods, professional communities, and social venues enabled him to compartmentalize relationships effectively while maintaining convincing personas tailored to each victim's specific circumstances and expectations.

Timeline analysis revealed periods of intense criminal activity alternating with apparent dormancy that likely corresponded to incarceration periods, relationship management challenges, or strategic planning for new campaigns. Court records and victim testimonies suggested that Jason's criminal activities intensified during economic pressures or personal crises while demonstrating remarkable consistency in methodology despite changing circumstances and evolving law enforcement awareness.

Communication methods evolved with technology advancement as Jason adapted his techniques to exploit new platforms, social media tools, and digital communication channels that provided enhanced opportunities for relationship development, victim surveillance, and identity management. His early adoption of emerging technologies gave him advantages over both victims and law enforcement agencies struggling to understand digital relationship dynamics and online fraud investigation techniques.

Financial impact assessment across multiple victims revealed total damages exceeding hundreds of thousands of dollars through various mechanisms including credit card fraud, identity theft, unauthorized account access, and direct financial manipulation disguised as loans or investment opportunities. Individual victim losses ranged from hundreds to tens of thousands of dollars, with emotional and psychological damage often exceeding quantifiable financial harm.

Law enforcement challenges became apparent through victim experiences with reporting processes, investigation procedures, and prosecution difficulties that reflected broader systemic issues in addressing romance fraud cases. Jurisdictional complications, evidence preservation problems, victim reluctance to participate in legal proceedings, and prosecutorial priorities that emphasized violent crimes over financial fraud created environments where romance criminals could operate with relative impunity.

Support network development among victims occurred organically as women discovered shared experiences through internet searches, media coverage, and informal communication channels that revealed patterns of victimization extending far beyond individual relationships. These connections provided emotional validation, practical assistance with legal proceedings, and collaborative efforts to warn potential future victims about ongoing criminal activities.

Media attention surrounding Jason Porter's criminal activities generated both positive and negative consequences for victims seeking justice and recovery. While publicity helped identify additional victims and raised awareness about romance fraud, it also exposed victims to public scrutiny, victim-blaming commentary, and privacy violations that complicated their healing processes and potentially discouraged other victims from coming forward.

Recovery challenges faced by victims extended far beyond financial losses to include trust issues, self-esteem damage, and relationship difficulties that persisted long after legal proceedings concluded. Professional counseling, support group participation, and peer connections with other victims became essential resources for rebuilding confidence and developing healthy relationship patterns that could withstand future manipulation attempts.

Prevention efforts emerged from victim experiences as women who had survived Jason Porter's manipulation became advocates for improved online safety education, enhanced dating platform verification procedures, and better law enforcement training for romance fraud investigation. Their collective voice contributed to broader conversations about digital relationship safety and criminal justice system responses to technology-enabled crimes targeting vulnerable populations.

# Chapter Eight

## From Victim To Vigilante

### Heather's Transformation: Making of a Digital Detective

Initial shock of discovering Jason Porter's true identity gave way to a burning determination that surprised even Heather herself as she channeled her professional skills into an investigation that would consume her thoughts, energy, and spare time for months. Rather than retreating into self-blame or denial as many victims do, Heather's real estate background had taught her to research thoroughly, verify claims independently, and pursue facts relentlessly until she understood every aspect of complex situations requiring careful analysis and strategic thinking.

Research methodology development began with Heather applying property investigation techniques to human behavior analysis, treating Jason's criminal history like a complicated title search that required examining multiple sources, cross-referencing information, and building comprehensive documentation that could withstand scrutiny. Her professional experience with due diligence processes, document verification, and background research provided a framework for investigating romance fraud that most victims lacked.

Digital literacy skills acquired through years of real estate marketing, social media management, and client research enabled Heather to navigate online databases, social media platforms, and public records systems with sophistication that exceeded typical amateur investigation capabilities. She understood how to use search engines effectively, interpret legal documents accurately, and organize information systematically for maximum impact and clarity.

Emotional compartmentalization became essential as Heather learned to separate her personal devastation from her investigative objectives, developing the ability to examine evidence objectively while processing trauma privately through professional counseling and trusted friend support. This psychological discipline allowed her to pursue justice without becoming paralyzed by anger or overwhelmed by the magnitude of betrayal she had experienced.

Networking expansion involved Heather reaching out to other victims, law enforcement officials, victim advocacy organizations, and legal professionals who could provide insights, resources, and collaboration opportunities that enhanced her individual efforts while building broader community awareness about romance fraud patterns and prevention strategies. These connections transformed her isolated victimization into collaborative justice-seeking that benefited multiple people.

Documentation systems establishment reflected Heather's professional training in maintaining detailed records, organizing complex information, and presenting findings clearly for various audiences including law enforcement, legal professionals, and media representatives. She created comprehensive files containing correspondence, financial records, photographs, and timeline documentation that provided irrefutable evidence of systematic deception and criminal activity.

Technology utilization involved Heather learning new digital tools for data analysis, evidence preservation, and communication coordination that enhanced her investigative capabilities while maintaining security and protecting other victims' privacy. Screen capture software, database management systems, and encrypted communication platforms became essential tools for professional-quality investigation work.

Legal system navigation required Heather to educate herself about criminal law procedures, evidence requirements, victim rights, and prosecution processes that would enable her to work effectively with law enforcement while understanding limitations and realistic expectations for justice outcomes. This legal education empowered her to advocate effectively for herself and other victims while avoiding unrealistic hopes that might lead to further disappointment.

Media engagement strategies evolved as Heather recognized that public awareness campaigns could serve multiple purposes including victim identification, predator exposure, and systemic change advocacy that extended far beyond her individual case. She learned to communicate effectively with journalists, maintain message consistency, and protect victim privacy while maximizing public education impact.

Psychological resilience building became an ongoing process as Heather developed coping mechanisms that allowed her to sustain intensive investigation work without compromising her mental health or professional responsibilities. Support group participation, therapy engagement, and self-care practices provided the foundation for long-term advocacy work that required emotional stamina and psychological stability.

## Building Case: Gathering Evidence and Finding Justice

Evidence collection began with Heather systematically documenting every aspect of her relationship with Jason Porter, including photographs, text messages, email correspondence, financial records, and witness statements that could establish timeline, demonstrate deception, and prove criminal intent. Her real estate background had taught her that thorough documentation was essential for successful legal proceedings and dispute resolution.

Financial analysis involved Heather working with banking professionals and forensic accountants to identify unauthorized transactions, fraudulent charges, and financial manipulation that might not be immediately apparent through casual review of account statements. This professional assistance revealed sophisticated fraud techniques that demonstrated Jason's criminal expertise while providing quantifiable damages for potential prosecution.

Witness identification required Heather to locate friends, family members, service providers, and other individuals who had interacted with Jason during their relationship and could provide testimony about his deceptive behavior, false identity claims, and manipulative techniques. These witnesses provided external verification of Heather's experiences while demonstrating pattern consistency that strengthened criminal cases.

Victim outreach involved Heather contacting women who had been identified through media coverage, court records, or personal investigation as potential Jason Porter victims, providing support, gathering additional evidence, and building collective action that enhanced individual cases while creating a broader impact than any single victim could achieve alone. This outreach required sensitivity and respect for other victims' privacy while maximizing collaborative potential.

Law enforcement collaboration presented ongoing challenges as Heather learned to work within police investigation procedures while advocating for thorough investigation and appropriate prosecution priorities. Her professional communication skills and comprehensive documentation helped establish credibility with detectives while demonstrating victim commitment that encouraged serious attention to romance fraud cases often dismissed as civil matters.

Legal strategy development involved Heather consulting with criminal attorneys, victim advocates, and legal aid organizations to understand prosecution requirements, evidence standards, and realistic outcomes for romance fraud cases within existing legal frameworks. This education enabled her to set appropriate expectations while maximizing chances for successful prosecution through strategic evidence presentation and witness coordination.

Media campaign management required Heather to balance public awareness goals with victim privacy protection, legal case integrity, and personal safety considerations that complicated publicity efforts while maximizing educational impact. She learned to work effectively with journalists while maintaining control over narrative development and protecting sensitive information that could compromise ongoing investigations.

Technology evidence preservation became crucial as Heather learned proper procedures for capturing digital evidence, maintaining chain of custody, and presenting electronic information in formats acceptable to courts and law enforcement agencies. Professional consultation with digital forensics experts ensured that evidence collection met legal standards while maximizing probative value.

Community education efforts expanded Heather's impact beyond individual justice seeking to include prevention programs, awareness campaigns, and policy advocacy that addressed systemic issues enabling romance fraud while supporting other victims and potential targets. Speaking engagements, media interviews, and educational materials development became vehicles for broader social change.

Systemic change advocacy emerged as Heather recognized that individual justice, while important, was insufficient to address underlying problems that enabled serial predators like Jason Porter to victimize multiple people with minimal consequences. Her advocacy work focused on improving law enforcement training, enhancing dating platform safety measures, and strengthening legal frameworks for romance fraud prosecution.

Personal healing integration required Heather to balance justice-seeking activities with recovery processes that addressed trauma, rebuilt trust, and restored emotional equilibrium necessary for healthy future relationships. Professional counseling, peer support, and self-care practices provided the foundation for sustainable advocacy work while facilitating personal growth and healing.

Long-term impact assessment revealed that Heather's transformation from victim to advocate had created lasting changes in romance fraud awareness, victim support systems, and law enforcement approaches that benefited countless individuals beyond her immediate case while establishing her as a respected voice in victim advocacy and criminal justice reform efforts.

# Chapter Nine

## *Legal Labyrinth*

### Prosecuting Romance Fraud: Why System Fails Victims

Criminal justice systems across Canada struggle with romance fraud cases because these crimes blur traditional boundaries between personal relationships and criminal activity, creating prosecution challenges that often leave victims feeling abandoned by legal institutions designed to protect them. Unlike violent crimes or property theft where criminal intent is clearly established, romance fraud requires prosecutors to prove deceptive intent within relationships that may have contained genuine emotional elements, making burden of proof significantly more complex than conventional fraud cases.

Evidence requirements for romance fraud prosecution demand documentation levels that many victims cannot provide because intimate relationships rarely generate the paper trails necessary for criminal court proceedings. Romantic partners typically communicate through private messages, share verbal agreements, and conduct financial transactions in informal settings that create minimal evidence suitable for courtroom presentation. Prosecutors need clear proof of criminal intent, financial damage, and systematic deception that can be difficult to establish when relationships evolve gradually over extended periods.

Jurisdictional complications arise frequently in romance fraud cases because perpetrators often operate across provincial or territorial boundaries while maintaining relationships with victims in multiple locations simultaneously. These geographic factors create coordination challenges between law enforcement agencies, complicate evidence gathering procedures, and enable criminals to exploit legal system boundaries that limit individual prosecutor authority and investigative resources.

Victim credibility becomes a central issue in romance fraud prosecution because defense attorneys routinely argue that alleged victims were willing participants in relationships who made poor financial decisions rather than criminal targeting. Cultural attitudes about personal responsibility, relationship choices, and financial decision-making influence jury perceptions and judicial attitudes that can undermine victim testimony while supporting defense narratives about consensual adult relationships rather than criminal exploitation.

Resource allocation within prosecutor offices typically prioritizes violent crimes and high-value financial fraud over romance cases that affect individual victims with relatively modest financial losses compared to corporate fraud or organized crime operations. Limited prosecutor time, investigative resources, and courtroom availability create environments where romance fraud cases receive minimal attention despite significant emotional and psychological impact on victims who desperately need legal validation and criminal accountability.

Plea bargaining procedures often result in reduced charges and minimal sentences that fail to reflect the full scope of romance fraud impact on victims or provide adequate deterrent effects for future criminal behavior. Prosecutors frequently accept guilty pleas to lesser charges rather than pursuing time-consuming trials that might result in acquittals, creating outcomes that leave victims feeling that justice systems minimize their suffering while enabling continued criminal activity.

Civil versus criminal distinctions create additional confusion for romance fraud victims who often receive advice to pursue civil litigation rather than criminal prosecution, despite civil courts being poorly equipped to address criminal behavior patterns that extend far beyond individual relationship disputes. Civil procedures require victims to finance their own legal representation while criminal activities demand law enforcement response and state-funded prosecution that many victims cannot access effectively.

Legal education gaps among law enforcement officers, prosecutors, and judicial personnel regarding romance fraud techniques and psychological impact create systematic under-response to cases that require specialized understanding of manipulation psychology, digital evidence analysis, and victim trauma patterns. Traditional legal training focuses on conventional crimes rather than emerging fraud methodologies that exploit emotional vulnerabilities through sophisticated psychological manipulation.

Sentencing guidelines for romance fraud often fail to account for multiple victim impact, long-term psychological damage, and criminal sophistication that distinguishes romance fraud from simple theft or conventional fraud cases. Judicial discretion in sentencing frequently results in penalties that reflect financial damages rather than comprehensive harm assessment including emotional trauma, trust destruction, and ongoing psychological consequences that affect victims for years after criminal prosecution concludes.

Legislative frameworks lag behind technological advancement and criminal methodology evolution, creating legal environments where existing statutes inadequately address sophisticated romance fraud techniques that exploit digital communication platforms, social media manipulation, and online identity creation tools. Lawmakers struggle to craft legislation that addresses emerging criminal techniques while preserving legitimate relationship privacy and personal autonomy rights.

**Porter Trials: Chronicle of Legal Frustration**

Initial charges against Jason Porter in 2012 reflected law enforcement understanding of his criminal activities at that time, resulting in twenty-three charges including fraud under five thousand dollars, breaking and entering, possession of property obtained by crime, and various credit-related offenses that captured only a fraction of his actual criminal enterprise scope and victim impact. These charges represented what prosecutors could prove definitively rather than comprehensive accountability for his romance fraud career.

Prosecution strategy development faced significant challenges as Crown attorneys attempted to present complex romance fraud evidence to juries unfamiliar with sophisticated manipulation techniques and psychological abuse patterns that distinguished Porter's crimes from conventional fraud cases. Prosecutors needed to educate court personnel about romance fraud methodology while simultaneously proving specific criminal acts that met legal standards for conviction beyond reasonable doubt.

Victim testimony coordination required prosecutors to prepare multiple women for court appearances that would expose their private relationship details to public scrutiny while reliving traumatic experiences under cross-examination designed to undermine their credibility and minimize Porter's criminal responsibility. Many victims expressed reluctance to participate in proceedings that felt like secondary victimization through legal processes that questioned their judgment and personal choices.

Defense strategy predictably focused on portraying Porter as someone who made poor relationship choices rather than a calculating criminal who systematically exploited vulnerable women for financial gain. Defense attorneys argued that romantic relationships involve complex emotional dynamics where financial support and gift-giving represent normal behaviors rather than criminal fraud, attempting to reframe criminal prosecution as inappropriate government interference in private relationship matters.

Evidence presentation challenges emerged as prosecutors attempted to demonstrate systematic criminal behavior patterns while working within legal frameworks designed for individual criminal acts rather than comprehensive fraud enterprises targeting multiple victims over extended time periods. Courts struggled to accommodate evidence volumes and victim testimony that exceeded typical criminal case parameters while maintaining fair trial procedures.

Plea negotiations resulted in Porter accepting responsibility for limited charges while avoiding trial proceedings that might have exposed the full scope of his criminal activities and their impact on victims seeking comprehensive accountability and public vindication. These negotiations reflected prosecutorial pragmatism about conviction probabilities while disappointing victims who wanted complete truth exposure through trial proceedings.

Sentencing outcomes consistently fell short of victim expectations and failed to reflect the comprehensive harm Porter had inflicted through years of systematic romance fraud targeting educated, successful women across Toronto. Judicial sentencing focused primarily on quantifiable financial damages rather than psychological trauma, trust destruction, and ongoing emotional consequences that continued affecting victims long after court proceedings concluded.

Appeal processes and subsequent charges created ongoing legal proceedings that extended victim involvement in criminal justice systems for years while Porter continued manipulating legal procedures to minimize consequences and delay accountability. Multiple court appearances, document preparation, and testimony requirements created additional burdens for victims seeking closure while managing personal recovery from criminal victimization.

Legal precedent establishment through Porter cases contributed to broader understanding of romance fraud prosecution challenges while highlighting systematic reforms needed to address sophisticated psychological manipulation crimes that exploit emotional vulnerabilities through extended relationship development. These cases influenced subsequent law enforcement training, prosecutor education, and judicial awareness about romance fraud impact and investigation requirements.

Systemic limitations revealed through Porter prosecution experiences demonstrated the need for specialized courts, trained personnel, and enhanced legal frameworks specifically designed to address psychological manipulation crimes that traditional criminal justice approaches handled inadequately. Victim advocates used these cases to promote legislative reforms and law enforcement policy changes that would better serve future romance fraud victims seeking justice and accountability.

# Chapter Ten

## *Psychology Of Predation*

**Inside Mind of a Romance Scammer: Expert Analysis**

Antisocial personality disorder characteristics manifest clearly in Jason Porter's criminal behavior patterns, demonstrating classic symptoms including persistent disregard for others' rights, systematic deceit for personal gain, and complete absence of genuine remorse for harm inflicted on victims. Mental health professionals who have studied romance fraud cases recognize that successful long-term deception requires psychological profiles that enable sustained manipulation without emotional interference from empathy or guilt that would prevent normal individuals from causing such comprehensive harm.

Psychological profiling conducted by forensic experts reveals that romance scammers like Porter typically possess above-average intelligence combined with exceptional emotional intelligence that enables them to read people accurately, identify vulnerabilities quickly, and adapt their approach to maximize effectiveness with specific targets. This cognitive combination creates predators who can analyze potential victims systematically while presenting personas precisely calibrated to exploit individual psychological needs and emotional desires.

Attachment disorder patterns stemming from Porter's childhood trauma created psychological foundations for viewing relationships as transactional opportunities rather than genuine emotional connections deserving of honesty and respect. Early abandonment experiences, parental loss, and institutional care environments taught him that emotional bonds were temporary at best and exploitative at worst, creating worldviews where manipulating others seemed like normal relationship behavior rather than criminal activity.

Narcissistic traits enable romance scammers to maintain grandiose self-images while viewing victims as inferior beings whose suffering is irrelevant compared to their own desires and needs. Porter's ability to justify his criminal behavior while maintaining positive self-concept demonstrates psychological mechanisms that allow predators to avoid cognitive dissonance that would prevent sustained criminal activity in individuals with normal empathy development and moral reasoning capabilities.

Compartmentalization skills represent perhaps the most disturbing aspect of romance scammer psychology because they enable criminals to separate their genuine personality from their criminal personas so completely that they can express apparent love and affection while simultaneously planning financial exploitation and emotional manipulation. This psychological splitting allows predators to maintain multiple relationships simultaneously without experiencing internal conflict about their deceptive behavior.

Manipulation expertise develops through practice and refinement as romance scammers learn to recognize emotional triggers, accelerate intimacy artificially, and maintain control over relationship dynamics that serve their criminal objectives. Porter's sophistication in reading body language, interpreting verbal cues, and responding to emotional needs demonstrates psychological skills that could have been channeled into legitimate helping professions but were instead weaponized for criminal exploitation.

Risk assessment capabilities allow successful romance scammers to evaluate potential victims for susceptibility factors while identifying threats that might expose their criminal activities or interfere with their manipulation strategies. Porter's ability to target specific demographic groups while avoiding individuals who might pose detection risks demonstrates criminal intelligence that extends far beyond simple opportunistic behavior into sophisticated predatory planning.

Emotional mimicry represents a crucial skill that enables romance scammers to appear genuinely caring and emotionally available while experiencing no authentic feelings for their victims. This psychological performance requires understanding emotional expression well enough to replicate appropriate responses without genuine emotional experience, creating relationships that feel authentic to victims while remaining completely artificial for perpetrators.

Justification mechanisms allow romance scammers to rationalize their criminal behavior through cognitive distortions that minimize victim harm, exaggerate victim culpability, and reframe criminal activity as justified responses to perceived unfairness or personal hardship. Porter's ability to maintain these justifications even when confronted with evidence of victim suffering demonstrates psychological defense mechanisms that protect criminal identity from moral challenges.

Pathological lying becomes second nature for successful romance scammers who develop abilities to create complex false narratives spontaneously while maintaining consistency across multiple relationships and extended time periods. This skill requires exceptional memory capabilities, creative storytelling abilities, and psychological comfort with deception that enables sustained criminal activity without detection through inconsistency or obvious fabrication.

## Perfect Storm: Why Smart Women Fall for Sophisticated Cons

Intelligence vulnerability paradox affects highly educated, professionally successful women who rely on analytical skills and logical reasoning that serve them well in career settings but become liabilities when confronting sophisticated emotional manipulation designed to bypass rational evaluation processes. Smart women often trust their ability to assess people accurately, making them more susceptible to predators who understand exactly how to exploit that confidence while presenting carefully crafted authenticity.

Emotional availability timing creates vulnerability windows when successful women reach life stages where professional achievements feel insufficient and romantic partnership becomes increasingly important for personal fulfillment. These transition periods, often occurring in thirties and forties, coincide with decreased patience for casual dating and increased willingness to invest deeply in relationships that promise genuine partnership and emotional satisfaction.

Professional isolation factors common among high-achieving women limit social circles to career-focused environments that provide minimal opportunities for organic relationship development, creating dependence on dating platforms where sophisticated predators operate most effectively. Professional demands that consume evenings and weekends further restrict natural meeting opportunities while generating emotional needs that romance scammers exploit through targeted availability and intensive attention.

Trust transfer mechanisms enable romance scammers to exploit professional women's business relationship skills by creating romantic connections that mirror successful professional partnerships built on mutual respect, shared goals, and collaborative problem-solving. Women who excel at building business relationships based on competence and reliability naturally extend these trust patterns to romantic partners who present appropriate professional credentials and relationship behaviors.

Caretaking instincts deeply embedded in many women's psychological profiles create vulnerabilities that romance scammers exploit through carefully revealed needs for emotional support, financial assistance, or personal guidance that generate protective responses and deeper emotional investment. Professional women often pride themselves on nurturing others' success, making them susceptible to partners who present opportunities for support and assistance that feel meaningful and appreciated.

Perfectionism pressures affecting high-achieving women create reluctance to acknowledge relationship problems or admit poor judgment that might reflect negatively on their self-image as competent decision-makers. This psychological pressure enables romance scammers to exploit victims' resistance to seeking outside perspective or acknowledging warning signs that might force uncomfortable self-evaluation about relationship choices.

Social expectation burdens place additional pressure on successful women to demonstrate romantic success that matches their professional achievements, creating environments where admitting relationship failure feels like acknowledging comprehensive life failure rather than simple romantic disappointment. These social pressures enable romance scammers to exploit victims' reluctance to end relationships that represent significant emotional and social investment.

Cognitive dissonance resolution processes allow romance scammers to exploit intelligent women's tendency to rationalize contradictory information rather than accepting that someone they love could be systematically deceiving them. Smart women excel at problem-solving and explanation-finding, making them particularly vulnerable to predators who provide plausible explanations for concerning behaviors while maintaining overall relationship satisfaction.

Resource accessibility makes professionally successful women attractive targets for romance scammers seeking financial gain while their emotional intelligence and communication skills create more satisfying manipulation experiences for predators who enjoy psychological dominance over accomplished individuals. These women represent both profitable targets and ego-gratifying conquests that serve multiple criminal motivations simultaneously.

Recovery challenges for intelligent victims often exceed those experienced by less educated targets because professional women face additional shame about being deceived despite their analytical capabilities and life experience. This enhanced embarrassment can delay help-seeking behavior, complicate legal reporting decisions, and create longer-lasting psychological impact that affects both personal recovery and professional confidence in ways that extend far beyond romantic relationship trauma.

# Chapter Eleven

## *Documentary Genesis*

### From Tragedy to Television: How a Story Found Its Voice

Media attention surrounding Jason Porter's criminal activities began generating public interest long before documentary producers recognized the broader storytelling potential embedded within this particular romance fraud case. Local Toronto news outlets had covered Porter's arrests and court proceedings since 2012, but these stories typically focused on immediate criminal charges rather than comprehensive examination of systematic victimization patterns or deeper social implications of romance fraud in digital age society.

True crime genre evolution during the late 2010s created entertainment industry demand for stories that combined criminal investigation with psychological analysis and social commentary, moving beyond simple procedural documentation toward comprehensive narrative exploration that engaged audiences intellectually and emotionally. Streaming platforms particularly sought content that examined criminal behavior within broader cultural contexts while providing educational value alongside entertainment appeal.

Heather Rovet's transformation from victim to advocate generated increasing media attention as her activism work, public speaking engagements, and victim outreach efforts demonstrated compelling narrative potential that extended far beyond typical criminal case coverage. Her articulate communication skills, professional background, and determined pursuit of justice created protagonist qualities that documentary producers recognized as essential for sustained audience engagement and meaningful social impact.

Industry networking through victim advocacy organizations, legal conferences, and media appearances gradually connected Heather with documentary professionals who understood the storytelling potential inherent in her experience while recognizing broader social relevance of romance fraud issues affecting increasing numbers of people navigating digital relationship landscapes. These initial conversations explored both personal story potential and broader educational opportunities that comprehensive documentary treatment could provide.

Executive producer involvement began when established documentary professionals recognized that Porter case represented a unique opportunity to examine romance fraud through multiple perspectives including victim experiences, criminal psychology, law enforcement challenges, and technological factors that enabled sophisticated deception in ways that traditional crime documentaries rarely achieved. This comprehensive approach appealed to producers seeking substantive content that could educate audiences while entertaining them.

Amazon Prime Video interest reflected streaming platform recognition that true crime content featuring strong female protagonists and contemporary social issues consistently attracted significant audience engagement while generating positive critical response and social media discussion that enhanced platform reputation and subscriber satisfaction. Romance fraud stories particularly resonated with female viewers who represented crucial demographic groups for streaming success.

Narrative development required careful balance between respecting victim privacy and creating compelling television that would maintain audience interest throughout multiple episodes while avoiding sensationalism that might exploit trauma for entertainment purposes. Producers needed to present complex criminal psychology and legal system challenges in accessible formats while honoring victim experiences and promoting educational awareness about romance fraud prevention.

Legal considerations demanded extensive consultation with entertainment attorneys, victim advocates, and law enforcement officials to ensure documentary production complied with privacy laws, defamation protections, and ongoing legal proceedings while maximizing storytelling impact and educational value. These legal constraints influenced narrative structure, interview approaches, and evidence presentation that balanced transparency with responsible journalism standards.

Victim consent processes required sensitive negotiation with multiple women who had experienced Porter's manipulation, ensuring voluntary participation while protecting those who preferred privacy and minimizing retraumatization through documentary production procedures. Producers needed to demonstrate genuine commitment to victim advocacy rather than exploitation while creating compelling content that served broader social education purposes.

Social impact potential attracted documentary team members who viewed this project as an opportunity to contribute meaningfully to public education about romance fraud while supporting victim advocacy efforts and promoting systemic changes that might prevent future criminal victimization. This mission-driven approach influenced production decisions, resource allocation, and promotional strategies that emphasized educational value alongside entertainment appeal.

## Behind Cameras: Creating "ROMCON: Who F*** Is Jason Porter?"

Production team assembly brought together experienced documentary professionals including director Henry Roosevelt, executive producers Toby Domer and Allison Brough, and co-executive producer Allyson Luchak, who combined expertise in crime documentaries, victim advocacy, and streaming platform content development. This collaborative approach ensured comprehensive coverage while maintaining sensitivity to victim experiences and educational objectives that distinguished this project from purely entertainment-focused productions.

Pre-production research required extensive investigation into court records, police reports, victim testimonies, and expert analysis that would provide factual foundation for documentary narrative while identifying key interview subjects, supporting evidence, and visual materials necessary for effective storytelling. Research team members spent months gathering documentation and verifying information that would support credible, comprehensive examination of Porter case and broader romance fraud issues.

Interview preparation involved careful coordination with Heather Rovet and other victim participants to ensure comfortable, supportive environments that would encourage honest, detailed testimony while minimizing retraumatization through production procedures. Producers worked with trauma specialists and victim advocates to develop interview protocols that prioritized participant wellbeing while gathering compelling content necessary for effective documentary impact.

Visual storytelling techniques incorporated dramatic reconstructions, archival footage, and stylized presentations that illustrated complex psychological manipulation processes and digital communication patterns in accessible formats that would engage audiences while educating them about romance fraud methodology. These visual elements required careful balance between dramatic impact and factual accuracy that respected victim experiences while creating compelling television.

Technical production challenges included presenting digital evidence, social media communications, and online dating platform interactions in formats suitable for television presentation while maintaining authenticity and educational value. Production team developed innovative approaches to visualizing digital relationships and virtual manipulation that had never been captured on film before.

Expert interview coordination brought together criminal psychologists, law enforcement specialists, victim advocates, and legal professionals who could provide authoritative analysis of romance fraud patterns while explaining complex psychological and legal concepts in language accessible to general audiences. These expert perspectives provided an educational framework that elevated documentary beyond simple crime stories into comprehensive social examination.

Editing process required careful narrative construction that balanced multiple victim stories, criminal background information, expert analysis, and social commentary into coherent two-part series that maintained audience engagement while delivering educational content and promoting victim advocacy goals. Editorial decisions influenced audience understanding and emotional response while respecting participant privacy and dignity.

Post-production refinement involved multiple review cycles with legal advisors, victim advocates, and subject matter experts who ensured factual accuracy, appropriate tone, and responsible presentation of sensitive material that could affect ongoing legal proceedings and victim recovery processes. These quality control measures protected all participants while maximizing documentary educational impact and social value.

Distribution strategy development focused on maximizing audience reach through Amazon Prime Video platform while coordinating promotional activities, media interviews, and educational outreach that would extend documentary impact beyond initial viewing audience. Producers collaborated with victim advocacy organizations and educational institutions to create supplementary materials that enhanced documentary educational value.

Festival premiere planning included world premiere at NXNE in Toronto, creating opportunities for community engagement, media coverage, and educational discussion that honored local victim experiences while promoting broader awareness about romance fraud prevention and victim support resources. Festival screenings provided platforms for continued advocacy work and community education initiatives.

Impact measurement systems tracked audience engagement, media coverage, victim feedback, and educational outcomes that demonstrated documentary effectiveness in achieving advocacy goals while informing future production decisions and continued outreach efforts. These assessment tools ensure accountability to victim participants and broader social education missions that motivated original production development.

# Chapter Twelve

## *Dissecting The Documentary*

### Frame by Frame: A Complete Guide to "ROMCON" Episodes 1 & 2

Episode structure planning for "ROMCON: Who the F*** Is Jason Porter?" follows established true crime documentary conventions while incorporating unique elements that distinguish this production from typical romance fraud coverage. As announced by Amazon Prime Video, the two-part series format allows comprehensive exploration of both Heather's personal journey and broader social implications of romance fraud in digital age dating culture.

Opening sequence development likely establishes Toronto as setting while introducing viewers to Heather Rovet's successful real estate career and personal life before her encounter with "Jace Peretti." Documentary conventions suggest that opening segments will create audience connection with Heather as protagonist while establishing stakes that make her subsequent victimization particularly devastating and relatable for viewers navigating similar relationship challenges.

First episode framework appears designed to chronicle relationship development from initial meeting through growing intimacy and eventual cohabitation, based on promotional descriptions emphasizing how "their relationship seemed perfect" for three years before "a shocking discovery revealed her lover was actually Jason Porter, a convicted criminal with a history of romantic deception". This narrative structure builds suspense while educating audiences about manipulation techniques that enabled sustained deception.

Interview integration throughout both episodes will likely feature "intimate interviews with Heather and other survivors" combined with "archival footage and dramatic reconstructions" that illustrate complex psychological manipulation processes without sensationalizing victim experiences. Production team's commitment to victim advocacy suggests careful balance between compelling storytelling and respectful treatment of trauma survivors.

Second episode focus appears to center on discovery process and aftermath, exploring how "Heather uncovers a disturbing pattern of manipulation and connects with other victims" while transforming "from heartbroken victim to determined investigator, risking everything to bring Porter to justice". This narrative arc emphasizes empowerment and agency rather than victimization, supporting broader documentary goals of education and advocacy.

Expert commentary integration will provide psychological analysis, legal context, and law enforcement perspective that elevates documentary beyond personal story into comprehensive examination of romance fraud as a social phenomenon. Production team's inclusion of mental health professionals, legal experts, and victim advocates suggests commitment to educational content that serves prevention and awareness purposes.

Visual storytelling techniques must address unique challenges of presenting digital relationships, online manipulation, and virtual deception in television format suitable for general audiences. Promotional materials mention "dramatic reconstructions" that will likely illustrate key relationship moments while protecting victim privacy and maintaining factual accuracy essential for credible documentary presentation.

Pacing considerations for two-part format require careful balance between maintaining audience engagement and providing comprehensive coverage of complex criminal behavior patterns spanning multiple years and numerous victims. Documentary structure must accommodate both entertainment value and educational objectives while respecting victim experiences and promoting meaningful social awareness.

## Truth vs. Drama

Documentary accuracy challenges begin with inherent limitations of any film adaptation of complex real-life events that occurred over multiple years and involved numerous participants with varying perspectives and memories. Even well-intentioned documentaries must compress timelines, simplify complicated relationships, and present selective evidence that fits narrative structure requirements while maintaining viewer engagement and educational value.

Victim representation authenticity will be a crucial factor in determining documentary success, particularly regarding how Heather Rovet's experience is portrayed in relation to other victims and broader patterns of romance fraud victimization. Responsible documentation requires avoiding sensationalism while accurately conveying psychological impact and manipulation sophistication that enabled Jason Porter's sustained criminal activity across multiple relationships.

Criminal psychology presentation poses significant challenges because documentary format cannot fully capture complex psychological profiles and manipulation techniques without risking oversimplification that might misinform audiences about romance fraud recognition and prevention. Expert analysis inclusion will be essential for providing accurate context while avoiding pseudo-psychological speculation that could mislead viewers about criminal behavior patterns.

Legal system coverage accuracy depends on the production team's understanding of Canadian criminal justice procedures, romance fraud prosecution challenges, and realistic outcomes for cases involving psychological manipulation and financial fraud. Documentary treatment of legal proceedings must balance viewer engagement with factual accuracy about complex legal processes that often disappoint victims seeking comprehensive justice.

Timeline compression inevitably affects documentary accuracy as three-year relationship development, discovery process, and legal proceedings must be condensed into two television episodes that maintain narrative coherence while providing sufficient detail for educational value. This compression may create misleading impressions about manipulation techniques, victim response patterns, or legal system timelines that differ significantly from actual experiences.

Digital evidence presentation requires innovative approaches to visualizing online relationships, social media manipulation, and virtual deception that maintain authenticity while creating compelling television content. Production team decisions about representing digital communications, dating platform interactions, and identity fraud techniques will significantly influence audience understanding of contemporary romance fraud methodology.

Emotional manipulation portrayal presents particular challenges because sophisticated psychological abuse techniques operate subtly over extended periods through relationship dynamics that may not translate effectively to visual media. Documentary treatment of emotional abuse requires sensitivity and expertise that protects victim dignity while educating audiences about manipulation recognition and resistance strategies.

Social context accuracy involves presenting romance fraud within broader digital dating culture without creating unnecessary paranoia or oversimplified prevention advice that fails to acknowledge complexity of modern relationship formation. Documentary responsibility includes promoting healthy skepticism while avoiding victim-blaming narratives that suggest preventable victimization through better judgment or increased caution.

Law enforcement representation should accurately reflect both capabilities and limitations of police responses to romance fraud while avoiding criticism or praise that misrepresents systemic challenges or individual officer dedication. Balanced coverage requires understanding institutional constraints, resource limitations, and training gaps that affect romance fraud investigation quality and prosecution success rates.

Victim advocacy impact assessment will ultimately determine documentary success in achieving broader social goals beyond entertainment value. Effective true crime documentation should promote victim support, criminal justice improvement, and prevention education while avoiding exploitation or sensationalism that benefits producers without serving affected communities or potential future victims.

Documentary legacy considerations include long-term impact on public understanding of romance fraud, victim support resources, and criminal justice system responses that may influence policy development, law enforcement training, and prevention program funding. Successful documentation creates lasting positive change that extends far beyond the initial viewing audience while supporting continued advocacy and education efforts.

Production ethics evaluation requires assessing whether the documentary creation process respected victim autonomy, protected participant privacy, and prioritized educational objectives over commercial success in ways that support broader victim advocacy goals while avoiding secondary victimization through media exploitation or sensationalized presentation of traumatic experiences.

# Chapter Thirteen

## *Aftermath And Legacy*

### Where Are They Now: Current Lives of Key Players

Heather Rovet continues operating her successful real estate practice in Toronto while maintaining active involvement in victim advocacy work that has become an integral part of her professional and personal identity. Her business motto, "Helping people find their perfect home or condo for the Next Chapter of their Life," has taken on deeper meaning as she assists clients while simultaneously supporting romance fraud survivors in rebuilding their lives after devastating betrayal and financial exploitation.

Professional growth following her traumatic experience has seen Heather develop specialized expertise in helping clients who are recovering from major life transitions including divorce, financial setbacks, and relationship trauma. Her personal experience with betrayal and recovery has enhanced her ability to provide compassionate, understanding service to clients facing similar challenges while maintaining professional boundaries that protect both her wellbeing and her business relationships.

Public speaking engagements have become regular features of Heather's advocacy work as she addresses professional associations, women's organizations, educational institutions, and law enforcement training programs about romance fraud recognition, prevention strategies, and victim support approaches. Her presentations combine personal testimony with practical education that helps audiences understand manipulation techniques while avoiding victim-blaming narratives that discourage reporting or help-seeking behavior.

Media participation continues as Heather works with journalists, documentary producers, and educational content creators to maintain public awareness about romance fraud while supporting other victims who need validation, resources, and encouragement to pursue justice or healing. Her willingness to share her story publicly has created a platform for broader education efforts while demonstrating the possibility of recovery and empowerment following devastating victimization.

Relationship status remains private as Heather focuses on personal healing, professional success, and advocacy work while managing ongoing trust issues and relationship anxiety that commonly affect romance fraud survivors. Friends and colleagues report that she has developed strong support networks while maintaining optimism about future relationship possibilities despite understandable caution about new romantic connections.

Jason Porter's current whereabouts and activities remain largely unknown to the public and his former victims, reflecting both his continued ability to avoid detection and legal system limitations in monitoring convicted romance fraud offenders after sentence completion. Court records and victim testimonies suggest he may continue criminal activities under different identities while law enforcement resources remain insufficient for comprehensive surveillance or prevention efforts.

Legal consequences for Porter's documented crimes resulted in relatively minimal sentences that failed to reflect comprehensive victim impact or provide adequate deterrent effects for future criminal behavior. His ability to serve limited jail time while returning to society without comprehensive rehabilitation or monitoring represents ongoing systemic failures in addressing sophisticated psychological manipulation crimes that cause extensive long-term damage to victims and communities.

Ongoing criminal investigation possibilities remain limited by jurisdictional complications, evidence preservation challenges, and resource constraints that affect law enforcement ability to pursue comprehensive prosecution for crimes spanning multiple years and numerous victims across different provinces. Recent victim reports suggest continued criminal activity, but verification and prosecution face familiar obstacles that have historically protected romance fraud perpetrators.

Family impact on Porter's children and relatives continues generating concern among victim advocates and social service professionals who recognize that his criminal behavior affects family members who may be unaware of his activities or unable to protect themselves from association with his ongoing crimes. Child welfare considerations and family court proceedings add complexity to criminal justice responses that must balance public safety with family protection.

Other victim outcomes vary significantly depending on individual circumstances, support systems, and recovery resources available to women who experienced Porter's manipulation and financial exploitation. Some victims have successfully rebuilt their lives and relationships while others continue struggling with trust issues, financial consequences, and psychological trauma that require ongoing professional support and community assistance.

Sarah, identified as Porter's first known victim, has reportedly moved forward with her life while maintaining privacy about her specific circumstances and recovery process. Her early cooperation with law enforcement and willingness to share her experience with subsequent victims demonstrated courage and community responsibility that contributed significantly to broader understanding of Porter's criminal patterns and victim impact.

Law enforcement personnel who investigated Porter cases have used their experience to develop enhanced training programs, improved investigation procedures, and better victim support protocols that benefit subsequent romance fraud cases. Detective Kent Hagerman and other officers involved in Porter investigations have become recognized experts in romance fraud investigation techniques and victim advocacy approaches.

Support network development among Porter's victims has created an informal community of survivors who provide mutual assistance, emotional support, and practical resources for recovery and advocacy work. These connections have proven invaluable for healing processes while contributing to broader victim advocacy efforts that extend beyond individual recovery to promote systemic change and prevention education.

**Digital Age Lessons: How One Woman's Story Changed Online Dating Safety**

Platform security improvements across major dating applications and websites have incorporated lessons learned from Porter case and similar romance fraud incidents, implementing enhanced verification procedures, improved reporting mechanisms, and better user education resources that help potential victims recognize manipulation attempts before significant emotional or financial investment occurs. These technological improvements represent direct responses to advocacy pressure generated by victim experiences and public awareness campaigns.

Education program development in schools, universities, and community organizations now regularly includes romance fraud awareness content that teaches digital literacy, psychological manipulation recognition, and healthy relationship boundaries that protect individuals from sophisticated predators operating through online platforms. Heather's story has become case study material used in these educational programs to illustrate both victimization risks and recovery possibilities.

Law enforcement training enhancement across Canada has incorporated romance fraud investigation techniques, victim advocacy approaches, and inter-agency cooperation protocols that improve criminal justice system responses to psychological manipulation crimes. Porter case analysis has contributed to specialized training programs that prepare officers to handle complex cases involving digital evidence, multiple victims, and sophisticated criminal methodology.

Victim support services expansion includes specialized counseling programs, legal advocacy resources, and financial assistance options specifically designed for romance fraud survivors who need comprehensive support addressing psychological trauma, legal proceedings, and economic recovery. These services represent recognition that romance fraud victims require specialized assistance different from other crime victim support programs.

Legislative advocacy efforts inspired by Porter case and similar incidents have promoted policy changes regarding romance fraud prosecution, victim protection, and criminal justice system procedures that better address psychological manipulation crimes. Victim advocates use specific case examples to demonstrate the need for enhanced legal frameworks that reflect contemporary criminal methodology and victim impact patterns.

Technology industry collaboration with victim advocates and law enforcement has produced improved safety features, enhanced user verification systems, and better fraud detection algorithms that identify suspicious behavior patterns before victims experience significant harm. Dating platform companies have implemented features directly responsive to concerns raised through cases like Porter's systematic exploitation of platform vulnerabilities.

Research contributions from Porter case have supported academic studies, criminal justice research, and psychological analysis that enhance professional understanding of romance fraud perpetrator psychology, victim vulnerability factors, and effective prevention strategies. Universities and research institutions use documented cases to develop evidence-based approaches to romance fraud prevention and victim support.

Public awareness campaigns utilizing Heather's story and similar victim experiences have reached millions of people through media coverage, social media education, and community outreach programs that promote romance fraud recognition while supporting victim advocacy goals. These campaigns balance prevention education with victim support messaging that avoids blame while promoting empowerment and help-seeking behavior.

Professional development programs for counselors, social workers, legal professionals, and healthcare providers now include romance fraud awareness training that enables better victim identification, appropriate support provision, and effective referral to specialized services. Porter case analysis contributes to professional education that improves service delivery across multiple disciplines.

International cooperation efforts have used Canadian romance fraud cases including Porter's activities to support cross-border law enforcement collaboration, information sharing protocols, and coordinated prevention efforts that address the global nature of online criminal activity. These cooperation initiatives recognize that romance fraud transcends national boundaries while requiring coordinated responses.

Social media safety education incorporates lessons from documented romance fraud cases to teach users about privacy protection, information verification, and communication safety that reduces vulnerability to manipulation while preserving benefits of digital relationship formation. Educational content balances caution with optimism about genuine connection possibilities.

Dating culture evolution reflects increased awareness of manipulation risks combined with maintained openness to legitimate relationship opportunities, demonstrating that effective education promotes healthy skepticism rather than relationship avoidance. Porter case contributes to cultural conversations about digital dating safety that support both prevention and authentic connection.

Long-term impact assessment reveals that individual victim advocacy can create lasting positive change extending far beyond personal recovery to influence criminal justice policies, technology industry practices, and social awareness levels that protect countless future potential victims. Heather's transformation from victim to advocate demonstrates the possibility of creating meaningful social change through personal courage and sustained commitment to community protection and education.

Manufactured by Amazon.ca
Bolton, ON

46091593R00096